THE REFORMATION
OF THE SIXTEENTH CENTURY

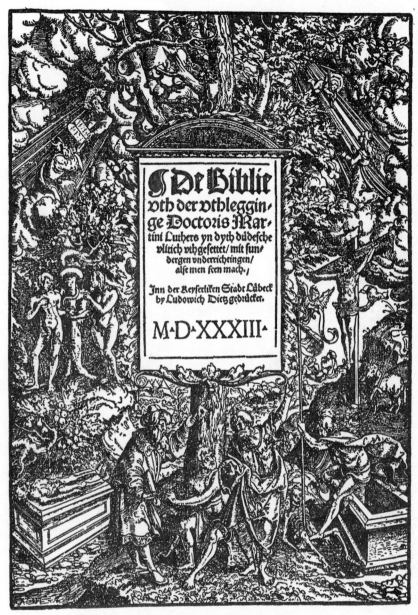

TITLE PAGE OF THE LOW GERMAN TRANSLATION
OF LUTHER'S BIBLE (1533)

The Reformation
of the Sixteenth Century

ENLARGED EDITION

ROLAND H. BAINTON

With a Foreword and Supplementary Bibliography
by Jaroslav Pelikan

BEACON PRESS • BOSTON

Beacon Press
25 Beacon Street
Boston, Massachusetts 02108

Beacon Press books are published under the auspices
of the Unitarian Universalist Association
of Congregations in North America.

First Edition published 1952. Enlarged Edition 1985
Printed in the United States of America

92 91   7 6 5 4

Library of Congress Cataloging-in-Publication Data

Bainton, Roland Herbert, 1894-
    The Reformation of the sixteenth century.

    Bibliography: p.
    Includes index.
    1. Reformation.   I. Pelikan, Jaroslav, Jan,
1923-   II. Title.
BR305.2.B298   1985   270.6   85-47516
ISBN 0-8070-1301-3

TO

DUDLEY AND DOROTHY PECK

VETERAN MISSIONARIES IN GUATEMALA

UNITED TO US IN THE BOND OF FAITH

AND THE SEED OF LIFE

Contents

Foreword

Jaroslav Pelikan

ALMOST TWENTY-FIVE YEARS AGO, in the autumn of 1960, I was invited to open conversations with the faculty and administration of Yale about the possibility of my becoming Titus Street Professor of Ecclesiastical History, to succeed Roland H. Bainton, who was nearing the statutory age of retirement and was therefore, legally speaking, "too old to teach." It was characteristically generous and self-effacing of him that, in one of a long series of postcards that we exchanged over the years, he paraphrased the words of John the Baptist in John 3:30: "Tu autem crescere debes, ego decrescere."

"Too old to teach," indeed! Roland Bainton went on teaching — not Yale students alone, but the world — for another two decades plus, maintaining an international travel schedule that would have crushed many a younger person, carrying on a correspondence in several languages that made his little notes and cartoons cherished collectors' items, and meeting publishers' deadlines (or, occasionally, missing them) with great good cheer. And even now when he cannot teach in person anymore, he goes on doing so through the remarkable library of volumes that he produced, both before and after his retirement. Some way to "decrescere"!

In that library of volumes, the best-known book is certainly his biography of Luther, *Here I Stand*, which remains

ix

unmatched even after the welter of books about Luther that came out of the five-hundredth anniversary of his birth in 1983. One of his own favorites was *Erasmus of Christendom*, in which the great humanist and scholar became visible as the world citizen and the protagonist of peace both civil and ecclesiastical. The most original contribution of Professor Bainton's scholarship is perhaps *Hunted Heretic*, his biography of Michael Servetus, published by Beacon Press, which put that enigmatic figure — opponent of the Nicene dogma of the Trinity, and predecessor of Harvey in the discovery of the circulation of the blood — into the context of sixteenth-century society and thought and helped students of every tradition see how heterogeneous and pluralistic a movement the Reformation was. (I cannot restrain the wish that Professor Bainton had added to his several Reformation biographies one on Ignatius Loyola, who was in so many surprising respects almost Luther's blood brother and who nevertheless became his bête noire.) But in some ways the most helpful of his books was *The Reformation of the Sixteenth Century*, also a Beacon book, in which he brought together into a single coherent account many insights and materials that could have remained scattered about in his monographs and specialized articles.

This book has stood for a third of a century as the place to begin a study of one of the most complex and controversial phenomena in the history of culture — not the place to end such a study, as Professor Bainton was the first to insist, but the starting point. It was, and is, marked by an impressive fairness and balance, as the author interprets with sympathy even positions and teachings he did not share or like. The careful and knowledgeable reader will indeed be able at times to tell "the good guys" from "the bad guys" in this account, but more often it will be evident that for Professor Bainton both groups were in fact "in-between guys." This is not because he lacked convictions. Both his passion about the cause of peace, to which I referred earlier in commenting on his biography of Erasmus, and his commitment to tolerance and religious liberty, documented in *The Travail of Religious Liberty*, come to expression as he narrates the development of one of the most intolerant and war-cursed periods in Western history.

Professor Bainton knew, better than most, that historical scholarship can never stand still, and he did his best, both through carrying on his own work and through encouraging that of his students and colleagues, to keep it moving. Inevitably, therefore, the scholarship of the past third-century has revised, supplemented, and sometimes even rejected the portrait of the Reformation of the sixteenth century painted here. An adequate account of those changes would require nothing less than a series of full-length monographs on the intellectual history of the 1950s, 1960s, 1970s, and 1980s. Monographs like that, continuing the histories of Reformation scholarship by such scholars as Roland Bainton's old comrade, the late Heinrich Bornkamm, as well as by John Dillenberger and Edgar Carlson, would be a valuable contribution to our understanding of how our picture of the past continues to be modified both by further research and by the events and experiences of our own time. Lacking any full-scale treatments of that dimension, we may nevertheless suggest at least three of the ways in which we have learned to see the Reformation differently, perhaps also to see it better.

When Professor Bainton wrote this book, only a few years after the conclusion of World War II, it was too early to recognize the full impact of the postwar political settlements on intellectual life, and specifically on Reformation scholarship. The redrawing of the map of Europe, including the division of Germany, put many of the major centers of Reformation scholarship under Marxist domination, for example, places such as Prague and Leipzig, where the history of the Reformation had been both enacted and written. Thus the journal *Luther,* which presents a regular summary of major research from all over the world, came to bear the address: "Institute for Church History, Karl Marx University, Leipzig, German Democratic Republic." Similarly, the definitive edition of the works of Jan Hus, discontinued during the War and the Nazi occupation, was resumed under the auspices of a Marxist academy of arts and sciences in the Czechoslovak Socialist Republic. Ever since Friedrich Engels himself and Karl Kautsky, with their books on the Peasants' War and on Reformation history, Marxists had been dealing with the Reformation, whose association with the rise of capitalism made it an essential chapter in their account of how European society has evolved. But now that, for the first time, Marxism has become the official ideology of states whose history was decisively shaped by the Reformation, the result has been an outpouring of scholarly work with which we must all come to terms. To mention only one example, Thomas Muentzer, to whom Bainton refers several times as one "whose major significance lies in the fathering of a new variety of theocracy," has been represented as almost a proto-Marxist, because of his battle against an entrenched feudalism in both church and state. If Professor Bainton could have written this book today, he would undoubtedly have much more to say about the chapters in the

story that are being illumined – and about those that are
being distorted – by this change of perspective.

Conversely, the past three decades have also witnessed a
massive revival of interest in the Reformation on the part of
Roman Catholic scholars. It is a strange feeling to recall that
this book was written before the Second Vatican Council –
an event in which the Roman Catholic Church took up many
of the themes of the Reformation, such as the vernacular
liturgy, the study of the Bible, and the universal priesthood
of all believers. Many observers, among them Roland Bainton, thought it was too little and too late, but one of the
results (and, I am sure, also one of the causes) of this
change of spirit was a change in the interpretation of the
Protestant Reformation. At the First International Congress
of Luther Research, which met in Aarhus, Denmark, in 1956,
there was a handful of Roman Catholic observers. By the
time the Fourth was convened, in Saint Louis, I had the
privilege, as its President, to welcome the Roman Catholic
scholars present as full-fledged participants and colleagues.
What is more, it was impossible to tell in the discussions
whether a particular scholar was a Roman Catholic or a
Protestant. The same is true increasingly of the scholarly
literature. The Reformers are no longer the exclusive possession of Protestant theologians: the Catholic tradition on
which they drew, often unconsciously, has become an essential component in our interpretation of their work. Erasmus,
for example, must now be seen as part of the Catholic Reformation, not simply, not even primarily, as part of the intellectual and scholarly background of the Protestant Reformation or as one of "the Free Spirits." And the elements of the
Catholic tradition in the teachings of the Protestant Reform-

ers themselves, whether Luther's doctrine of the real presence in the Eucharist or Calvin's doctrine of the Trinity, cannot be dismissed as vestigial remnants that they should have sloughed off, but must be interpreted as fundamental components of their faith and thought. As Protestant and Roman Catholic scholars work together on the history of the Reformation, all sorts of exciting — and embarrassing — insights are sure to appear.

A third change in the history of Reformation history is related to the second but is by no means identical with it: the rediscovery of the connections, and of the contrasts, between the Reformation of the sixteenth century and the intellectual, cultural, and theological movements of the fourteenth and fifteenth centuries. It was almost two and a half centuries from the death of Thomas Aquinas to the emergence of Martin Luther, but both to most Reformation scholars and to most medievalists that period has remained largely uncharted territory. Significantly, for example, this book does not even mention Gabriel Biel (d. 1495), the Tübingen theologian whose thought was a dominant force in Luther's day, and it refers only once to William of Occam. During the past decades, however, scholars have been hard at work to correct that underemphasis. Critical editions, scholarly monographs, and large-scale histories have begun to appear, revising forever our grasp of the dynamics of the Reformation. By a change of nomenclature paralleling the one in Leipzig mentioned earlier, the "Institute for Reformation History" at the University of Tübingen is now called "Institute for Reformation and the Late Middle Ages." It is still too early to tell what the outcome of all this work on the later Middle Ages will do to Reformation study, but it is safe to say that both the sources of Reformation thought and the objects of Reformation polemic will become more visible, and that what has been called (by Heiko A. Oberman) "the pregnant plurality of fourteenth-century thought" will be seen both as a source of the thought and as an object of the polemic.

Eventually, therefore, it will not be enough to add such a foreword as this, together with a brief bibliography, to Roland Bainton's *Reformation of the Sixteenth Century,* and a totally new introduction to Reformation history will have to be written. But for now, the remarkable feature of this book is not how much new would have to be added to bring it up to date, but how up to date so much of it remains. Like its author of blessed memory, it is still not "too old to teach."

Illustrations

_____

The author wishes to express his gratitude to Miss Olive Sarber for preparing the index.

THE REFORMATION
OF THE SIXTEENTH CENTURY

Introduction

THE REFORMATION OF THE SIXTEENTH CENTURY occurred at a
time of so many upheavals that the period is often regarded
as the transition from the Middle Ages to modern times.
A number of movements coincidently flourished. The
Renaissance shifted interest from heaven to earth, while
geographical expansion enlarged the known earth. The
Renaissance manifested more enthusiasm for classical than
for Christian antiquity, while at the same time nationalism
enfeebled the Holy Roman Empire and weakened the papal
theocracy. The corporate guild system of the Middle Ages
in the meantime was disintegrated by the economic individualism of incipient capitalism which simultaneously developed banking and fostered big business. In the midst of
this ferment the Reformation shattered the monolithic structure of the Holy Catholic Church.

The Reformation was not derived from any of these other
movements, however much its course may have been conditioned by them. With some it could form alliances, to
some it was unalterably opposed. And if it abetted them at
all by weakening churchly controls, such was not the intent.
The Reformation was above all else a revival of religion.
So much is this the case that some have looked upon it as
the last great flowering of the piety of the Middle Ages.
In consequence these interpreters are disposed to date the
modern age in the field of religion rather from the En-

lightenment of the eighteenth century than from the Reformation of the sixteenth. With justice they point out that the Reformation was intensely preoccupied with the world to come, viewed all life under the aspect of eternity, throbbed to the Christian drama of redemption, subordinated even political alliances to the truth of God, was intolerant of dissent, credulous of superstition, addicted to belief in demonology and witchcraft, often millenarian and sometimes Messianic. In all these regards the Reformation was the last upsurging of the religion of the Middle Ages.

On the other hand the Reformation manifestly split the ecclesiastical structure of the Middle Ages and thereby shattered the framework of that society called Christendom, resting on one faith and one baptism, owing allegiance to one church focused in Rome, distinct from the empire of the second Rome at Constantinople or the third at Moscow, and of course from the realm of the infidel Turk. This Christian society was compared to the seamless robe of Christ — and that robe was rent by the Reformation. At this point the Protestant movement appears as the great disintegrator of medieval Catholicism.

But if the sight be shifted from the ecclesiastical structure to the sense of religious concern, the Reformation may be regarded as the renewer of Christendom. In the age of the Renaissance the Catholic Church had been so far secularized that even the popes did not disdain to make alliances with the unbelieving Turk against the believing monarchs of Europe. The Reformation made religion and even confessionalism a paramount issue in politics for another century and a half.

The reformers of the sixteenth century were themselves not unmindful of the problem of their relation to that which

went before and that which was to come. They thought of
themselves indeed as rebels but not as innovators, and in
fact leveled the charge of innovation against the Church
which had cast them out. Martin Luther claimed on occasion that the Church against which his critique was directed
was only four hundred years old. The papal theocracy alone
was the object of his attack, and his effort was to restore the
Church of the early Middle Ages. On occasion, however, he
would carry the fall in church history back to the eighth
century which he conceived as the period of the rise of
the temporal power of the popes. And in that case the
church to be restored would be that of St. Augustine or even
better of Paul and the Gospels. The essential note was the
recovery of uncorrupted Christianity.

To understand this point of the reformers one needs to
keep in mind the main outlines of the development of the
Church up to their time. A swift sketch is therefore in
order. The first period was of course the age of persecution
prior to Constantine when the Church grew by witnessing,
neither aided nor hampered by an alliance with the state.
The second period was that of the Church in the Roman
Empire when already the concept of a Christian society was
envisaged, and the collaboration commenced between the
two powers by which it was to be directed — namely the
Empire and the Church. With the adoption of Christianity
the emperors abandoned the claim to deification and relinquished also any status in the ecclesiastical hierarchy, but
by way of compensation became in a sense lay bishops. In
the East a system developed where the affairs of the Church
were subject to imperial control and the sphere of the Church
was severely restricted. Not politics and social reform but
worship in the churches and contemplation in the monas-

teries became the pattern of Byzantine Christianity, commonly denominated the system of Caesaropapism because the Caesar at many points operated as the pope.

In the meantime a variant development was commenced in the West when the barbarian invasions broke up the unity of the state and gave to the Church a unique opportunity. The Church then inherited the mantle of the Caesars and became herself the integrator, educator, and civilizer of the invaders. The Church solemnized the marriage between the northern and southern cultures and undertook to allay the feuds of turbulent tribes more disposed to turn Christ into a god of battles than to recognize each other as brothers.

Three periods are discernible in medieval church history: dissemination, domination, and disintegration. The first may be taken roughly from the fifth through the eleventh century; the second approximates the twelfth and thirteenth; the third, the fourteenth and fifteenth centuries.

The beginning was marked by the dissemination of orthodox Christianity among the Arian and pagan barbarians, until Roman Christianity had penetrated to the Slavic border and won the allegiance of the Scandinavian countries. Along with dissemination went the effort to permeate society with Christian faith and ideals, but in the process the Church became so intimately involved that the leaven was in danger of being lost in the lump. There was no other way, because the society which emerged as the invasions subsided was agrarian, trading in kind rather than in coin. Missionaries could not be financed from Rome and were driven in consequence to discover means of self-support. The only possibility was to possess and till the soil. The Church thereby became a great landed institution, owning as much as half of the territory in France and Germany.

In a culture where all institutions rested on land, the Church found herself an integral part of the feudal system — and she was secularized in the process. The barbarians were a lusty breed, contemptuous of the meek, and mass conversions served less to elevate them than to dilute the Church.

Corruption set in and it affected all the agents of the Church engaged in the winning of the West. Of these there were three types: the popes, the priests, and the monks. When government collapsed, the papacy was able by reason of its vast resources to step into the breach and take over many of the functions hitherto exercised by the state, such as feeding the populace of Rome, ransoming prisoners, and making treaties with the invaders. By the eighth century the Church had become not only a propertied but also a political power. This was the point at which Luther located the first fall in the history of the Church. As soon as the popes came to be sovereigns, they were involved in entanglements with other sovereigns and differed from them little, either in faith or in deportment.

The second great institution was that of the secular clergy, so called because they operated in the world. These were the parish priests and the bishops. Their contacts with the people were intimate and their possessions vast. So closely were they geared into the feudal structure that some bishops were at the same time lords — "prince bishops," they were called. One of them flippantly remarked that as a bishop he was celibate, as a baron he was married and the father of a numerous family. The secularization of the parish clergy became scandalous.

Somewhat better was the situation of the third great institution, namely monasticism, because the monks lived in segregated communities and enjoyed a measure of independence. It is therefore no accident that reformatory movements commonly emanated from monasteries. But the monks, too, lived from the soil, owned and controlled the soil, and were subject to all the temptations which property entails. If monastic lands were overrun by marauders the abbots put armor over their cowls, as the bishops did over their cassocks. Prosperity itself corrupts. A medieval monk formulated the law of the monastic cycle: "Discipline begets abundance, and abundance, unless we take the utmost care, destroys discipline; and discipline in its fall pulls down abundance."

By the twelfth century reform was universally conceded to be grievously needed. Then came the second stage in the attempt to Christianize society, this time not so much by permeation as by domination. The Church became not merely a temporal power but a theocracy. The movement which effected the change originated in a monastery but is named Gregorian, after Pope Gregory VII, who espoused its program to reform alike the monasteries, the Church, and the world. The monasteries were to be reinvigorated by the revival and stiffening of the Benedictine rule. The Cluniacs and Cistercians exemplified the new spirit. Civil society was to be Christianized in that the laity should cease devouring one another and make of their fighting a seasonal and restricted sport: such was the program of the *Peace* and the *Truce* of God. Or, if they must fight, they should not exterminate each other but rather take service under the banner of the Church against the enemies of the faith. Here was the origin of the idea of the crusade. The theocracy was taking shape.

If it were to be realized, the parish church must be pure,

THE POPE AND CARDINALS IN CONCLAVE

and purity was taken to mean that the clergy should be celibate like monks. An additional consideration was that the priesthood should not become an hereditary caste. Therefore in the eleventh century the papacy undertook to impose the rule of celibacy on all the clergy.

At the same time the Church must be free — that is to say, independent of lay control. The request would have been the more readily granted if the Church had not come to be so intimately enmeshed in the whole social and political structure. In a society where all relations rested on land and the Church was the most landed of all institutions, the rulers naturally wished to be sure that the incumbents would discharge all of the normal obligations, and for that reason demanded the right to review appointments. The civil rulers also at times conceived of themselves as the lay representatives of a Christian society empowered to discipline the spiritual branch if recreant to duty. Out of zeal for the Church, kings and emperors sometimes deposed popes. Such interference, however highly motivated, the Church would not brook.

The only alternative was that the Church must be dominant. Leadership must rest in ecclesiastical hands. Thus arose the papal theocracy. The ground on which it rested was the sacramental system. The Church claimed to be the director of society not by reason of the goodness of churchmen but by virtue of the prerogative of the clergy alone to celebrate the sacraments, through which exclusively salvation is mediated to men. Baptism, the first of the sacraments, washes away all previous sin, confers membership in a Christian community, is ineradicable, and confers rights over the children of the baptized, even though the baptism be subsequently repudiated, as sometimes happened after forced conversion; baptism was conferred upon every child born into the community, who by that token became also a member of the Christian Church. Marriage was a sacrament under ecclesiastical jurisdiction. Penance insured the forgiveness of sins as often as they might be committed and confessed. The sacrament of the Mass conferred union with God and eternal life. Extreme unction on the point of death was the final seal in the cycle of redemption. No layman could perform any one of these rites. For that reason the meanest priest was greater than the loftiest emperor. The latter could confer on man only tranquillity on earth. The former could convey the peace of heaven. The priest enjoyed this power by virtue of another sacrament controlled also exclusively by the Church, the sacrament of ordination. Hence the cleavage between the laity and clergy; hence the claim of the clergy to be the directors, if not the rulers, of society. Whereas in the Carolingian period the king had been regarded as the Lord's anointed to serve God through the state, in the Gregorian period the tendency was to disparage the state and to minimize the office of the king as concerned only with the temporal end of man. The medieval theocracy reached its peak in the thirteenth century under Innocent III. No monarch in Europe was so powerful. Though he made no pretence of ruling outside of the papal states as a direct temporal lord, he did claim to judge of sin, and there was always enough sin to enable him to judge everything. Actually he was the arbiter of Europe. With spiritual weapons alone he held sway from Gibraltar to Jerusalem, from Stockholm to Constantinople, as the vice-regent of Christ and shepherd of the faithful.

The external triumph of the Church was accompanied by an imposing synthesis in the realm of thought at the hands of Thomas Aquinas, who gathered up the threads from Christian and classical antiquity, from the wisdom of the Arabs and the philosophy of the medieval Jews into an integrated theological system. The assimilation of these non-Christian elements was facilitated by a scheme of ascending levels rising from human reason to divine revelation, with no sharp rift anywhere along the line because revelation is reasonable. The same scheme of ascents was used to justify the feudal system and the ecclesiastical hierarchy and in turn to subordinate the state on a lower level to the Church on a higher. Still more significant was the metaphysical support given alike to the Empire and the Church by regarding them as the concrete manifestations of super-terrestrial entities and not mere aggregates of individuals. Reality itself was conceived in corporate terms as comprising great "universals" and not as consisting only of unrelated single items. This philosophy called "realism" planted state and Church in the realm of ultimate being.

Before the Reformation the disintegration of this stupendous structure of theocracy and theology had already set in. Without and within came decline. The papacy was speedily undone by its very successes in weakening the empire and in building up the emerging national states. The ruling dynasty in the Holy Roman Empire, the House of Hohenstaufen, was shattered by papal manipulations, while France grew into the semblance of a modern state with papal assistance.

Then the Church first was worsted in a conflict with incipient nationalism in France. The occasion arose from a change in the economic structure of society. In the wake of the crusades, commerce was revived and coincidently money returned as a medium of exchange. The finances of the Church shifted from revenue in kind to revenue in coin. Then the king of France forbade any exportation of gold to Rome. The papacy went bankrupt and in consequence was transferred from Rome to Avignon on the confines of France, there to remain for a period described as the Babylonian Captivity, corresponding roughly to the ancient captivity of the Jews for seventy years. The Avignon period, to be exact, was from 1305 to 1378. During that time the popes were all French.

Papal finances had to be reorganized completely with the loss of the Italian estates, and the popes of Avignon, notably

Pope John XXII, invented and exploited every device for extracting money alike from the faithful and from the local churches and abbeys for the coffers of the papacy. The rule was introduced that whenever a bishop was appointed, the first year's income — called an *annate* — should go to the pope. To fill a vacancy a bishop was often transferred from another see and another vacancy was thus created. Or perhaps the appointment would be deferred and the pope would appropriate all of the income in the interim; this was called a *reservation*. Before a benefice actually became vacant a prospective claimant might for a fee be granted an expectation. Fees abounded and special offices were devised in order to be sold.

The most lucrative expedient proved to be that of indulgences. The practice arose during the crusades of granting to soldiers who embarked on the holy war all of the remission of penalties which might have been theirs had they stayed at home and performed the satisfactions required by the penitential system. The next stage was to confer like benefits upon those who, unable to go on the crusade, contributed to the enterprise. The object could easily be expanded, and in time indulgences were dispensed in order to raise money for the construction of hospitals, bridges, cathedrals, and all manner of public works. The underlying theory was that Christ and the saints had more merits than were needful for their own salvation. The superfluous credits were stored in a treasury placed by God at the disposal of the popes and capable of transfer to those whose sins were in arrears. Precisely how much could be conferred was under debate. The more moderate opinion was that the pope could remit only those penalties which he had himself imposed on earth. Others held that his jurisdiction extended to the dead in purgatory whose term could be reduced and perhaps even completely canceled. The most extravagant pretensions held that the pope might in this way remit not only penalties but also forgive sins. The claims continued to mount. The most unqualified were not more than fifty years old in Luther's day, and the particular instance of the indulgence traffic against which he protested marked the peak of the pretensions.

By all these devices the popes at Avignon succeeded in collecting an income three times that of the king of France. One may wonder that the monarch who would not permit a sou to go to Rome should have allowed so much to reach Avignon. He would scarcely have done so had he not profited by exercising control over the papacy. But by the same token other nations grew restive. England in the days of Wyclif and John of Gaunt meditated throwing off the papal yoke, and the emperor in Germany was for thirty years under an interdict. The resentment was all the greater because the pope spent 63 per cent of his enormous income on wars for the recovery of his lost Italian estates. The disquiet was so great that the formation of national churches might easily have been advanced by two hundred years had not the pope returned to Rome.

Thereupon, however, the cardinals refused to leave Avignon and elected another pope. The Roman pontiff retorted by creating a new college of cardinals. The papal schism that ensued lasted from 1378 to 1417. In order to restore the shattered unity, Church councils were summoned. The sponsors hoped not merely to eliminate the double papal line but also to curb the monarchical tendencies in the ecclesiastical structure in favor of a constitutional monarchy. They hoped also to correct many abuses in the life of the Church.

The financial exploitations were crying for redress. So also were the moral corruptions, inasmuch as the imposition of celibacy had resulted in some quarters in the prevalence of clerical concubinage. This of course was not universally true; many priests kept their vows. Nevertheless on the eve of the Reformation clerical concubinage was a recognized system condoned by the laity and taxed by the Church. The councils did succeed in ending the schism; they did not succeed in reforming the Church.

The popes, when the schism was over, regained and intensified their monarchical position, and a pope shortly before Luther's day branded an appeal to a council without papal consent as constituting in itself a case of heresy. The more the Church diminished in prestige and power, the more its own organization was centralized and its claims intensified. The assertion that the two keys alike of spiritual and civil power belong to the pope goes back not to the days of Innocent III, when the affirmation came nearest to being true, but to the days of the debacle. After the schism and in the period of the Renaissance, the papacy emerged as something between an Italian city-state and a European power, without forgetting at the same time the claim to be the vice-regent of Christ. The pope often could not make up his own mind whether he was the successor of Peter or of Caesar. Such vacillation had much to do with the rise and success, not to mention the necessity, of the Reformation.

The fifteenth century brought new currents in the intellectual and religious spheres. The great theological synthesis of Thomas Aquinas disintegrated coincidently with the decline of the papacy. The late Scholastics lost faith in the intelligibility of reality because they relinquished the metaphysical unities. For them reality was held to consist of unrelated particulars. Church and state are not antecedent entities but simply contractual associations. The church then becomes a voluntary society, the state a compact, and marriage similarly a contract. Here is the philosophy of individualism undercutting the great unities well in advance of the Reformation. Certain theological dogmas also were undercut, for if reality consists of unrelated individuals, then the three persons of the Trinity must be three gods. Nevertheless the doctrine of the Trinity was retained on the ground that what is true for philosophy need not be true for theology. But in that case theology, with no philosophical undergirding, can rest only on authority. The tendency of the papacy to make more pretentious claims as its power waned was also paralleled by the recourse in theology to authority when the grip on truth was relaxed.

The period of the Renaissance in the late fifteenth century came close to confronting the Church with a rival view of life. During the fifteenth century the revival of commerce and urban life produced in Italy a galaxy of brilliant city-states which contrived to preserve a balance of power between themselves and to avoid becoming the cockpit of the rivalries of the great European powers. In this unusual setting a new class emerged of scholars and artists, not members of monastic orders. Their ideal was the exploration of all learning and all skills. The universal man, the *uomo universale*, essayed to excel in sport, art, literature, exploration or war. Every department of life should be subject to the rational control of man; the stress was laid in art on perspective, in statecraft on diplomacy, in business on bookkeeping, and in war on strategy. The life to come was not necessarily excluded from the purview, but obviously the emphasis was comparatively this-worldly. Among the areas to be explored

were alike the new worlds beyond the seas and the learning
of classical antiquity. This revival of the ancients was not
necessarily inimical to Christianity. A synthesis of the classical and Christian had been achieved previously by Augustine
and Aquinas, but the tendency to incorporate into Christianity alien elements or even to make of Christianity only a
religion among religions was obviously disruptive. The
popularity of Cicero was perhaps the most subversive because he was so near to the Kingdom, inasmuch as he believed in God, immortality, justice, and magnanimity. But
naturally he knew not Christ and his ethic was that of an
eclectic Stoicism. Delving in ancient texts at the same time
sharpened the methods of historical criticism to the point
that certain documents crucial for papal pretensions were
exposed as spurious, such as the forged "Donation of Constantine." Yet no overt clash occurred between the Renaissance and the Church — save for one minor fracas in
Germany over Hebrew studies — and the reason was that
the popes themselves became the patrons of the new learning. The Renaissance invaded the Vatican.

A brief glance at a few of the Renaissance popes will serve
to illustrate many of the characteristics of the period. Sixtus
IV was a despot of an Italian city-state who did not suffer
his right hand as the vicar of Christ to be too inquisitive
about the doings of his left hand as the prince of the Eternal
City. He was a patron of the arts and gave his name to the
Sistine Chapel. Alexander VI was a rake whom Catholic historians regard as an unspeakable disgrace. His misdemeanors, however, are not suffered to discredit the claims of
the Church because the office is distinguished from the
man and infallibility does not rest on impeccability. His-
torically speaking the amours of Alexander VI reveal that

the failure of the Gregorian reform to establish clerical celibacy extended to the very citadel of the Church. Julius II was very different, chaste, imperious, a pope in arms, a relic of crusading days, who led his own troops in the conquest of Bologna, a man of magnificence who discovered the artists Bramante, Raphael and Michelangelo and inaugurated the construction of the new St. Peter's. Leo X was a Medici, indolent, elegant, skilled in impromptu Latin orations, a spendthrift who squandered more on pageants and gambling than on the needs of the Church or the patronage of the arts. That such a trifler should have occupied the See of Peter at a time of crisis is regarded by Pastor, the great Catholic historian, as a supreme calamity. To hold the Reformation responsible for the destruction of the great papal theocracy of the thirteenth century is to forget the condition into which it had already fallen.

The decline did not come without protest or effort at reform. The four hundred years preceding the Reformation had been characterized not only by the disintegration of the papal power and the accentuation of papal claims, but also by the rise of sectarian movements splitting off from the Church. The sectarian urge in the earlier Middle Ages had found an outlet in missions and monasticism, but in the twelfth century the very reformatory zeal which created the theocracy produced also the protests against its inadequate achievements. The peace movement had issued in a crusade, monastic poverty by frugality amassed wealth, clerical celibacy fostered clerical concubinage. Indignant reformers concluded that if correction on a universal scale were no more successful, the attempt must be renewed with select units of those personally committed. The outcome was a proliferation of sects in southern France and northern

Italy. The Rhine valley and the Netherlands were swept by mystical movements. Bohemia seethed with unrest in which heresy fused with national feeling.

The sectarian movements were reinforced by subversive ideas, one of which was eschatology, a revival of the early Christian expectation of the speedy return of Christ. His coming would be preceded by the reign of Antichrist, who must be overthrown before the advent of the new dispensation. The very concept of the end of the age was subversive to the security of a great ongoing institution like the medieval Church. But if in addition the head of that institution were identified with Antichrist, revolution was then afoot. The sects identified Catholic Rome with the Babylon of the Apocalypse.

Another and perhaps still more disruptive notion was the view that the church on earth is not the true Church of God, which consists only of the elect, predestined from the foundation of the world. If the elect cannot be identified the idea is not subversive, but if morality be the touchstone the inference is obvious that an immoral pope is neither the head of the Church nor even a member. Predestination and millenarianism were sometimes combined and the Church as an earthly institution was then undercut both from before and from behind. These ideas flourished among the Wyclifites and Hussites and in a measure also among the Fraticelli, a schismatic branch of the Franciscans.

The most devastating attack on the structure of the Church came from a denial of the efficacy of the sacraments or of priestly power to dispense them. The Church had declared at the great Lateran Council under Innocent III that the priest by pronouncing the words, "This is my body," effects the miracle of transubstantiation, by which the bread and wine are changed into the body and blood of God. Wyclif denied that the change takes place and in this he was followed by Hus. Other sectaries contended that the virtue of the sacrament cannot be communicated by an evil priest. Either of these views demolished sacerdotalism by discrediting sacramentalism.

The piety of the Church throughout this period was by no means moribund. In the hamlets all over Europe there was more of simple faith and godly living than the annalists saw fit to record. We do know of groups, more or less informal, gathered to cultivate the interior life. The Friends of God in the Rhine Valley and the Brethren of the Common Life in Holland engaged in very little overt attack on current abuses, but they set an example by cultivating the imitation of Christ, the submergence of the self in the ocean of the Godhead, and the service of man in joyful suffering after the manner of the crucified Lord. These sects are not the immediate progenitors of the Lutheran reform but they contributed ideas — notably to the left wing of the Reformation.

The lineaments also of the Catholic Reformation were sketched before the Evangelical reform emerged. The Catholic movement was characterized by orthodoxy in faith and asceticism in conduct. Alike the doctrinal beliefs and the moral demands should be enforced. The discipline should be applied from the top down. Spain, fiercely orthodox because of the conflict with the remnants of the Moors and Jews, was the center of the movement. Cardinal Ximenes was the first great exemplar, a curious combination, a barefoot Franciscan and a cardinal, a crusader in arms and a friar in a hair shirt, a grand inquisitor and a Renaissance scholar, chancellor of the realm and rigid disciplinarian. He

anticipated certain elements in the program of the Jesuits
and the so-called Counter Reformation.

This is a very brief sketch of the emergence and decline
of the papal theocracy and the scholastic synthesis. As
power waned, claims increased. When the papacy was no
longer spontaneously recognized as the arbiter of Europe,
affirmations of 'universal jurisdiction became more absolute.
When the gifts of the faithful no longer flowed unsolicited
into the coffers of the Church, money-raising devices were
heavily exploited. When philosophy no longer easily undergirded faith, authority was the more exalted.

This was the situation on the eve of the sixteenth century.
All serious spirits were disturbed and recognized the need
for reform. But one party wanted to go back to the heyday
of the high Middle Ages when the new monastic orders
flourished and the papacy wielded theocratic power. Such
was the ideal of the Catholic Reformation. Others felt that
theocracy and monasticism at their very best constituted
abuses, and the return must be to the simplicity of a much
earlier time. This was the view of what came to be known
as the Protestant Reformation.

1

Luther's Faith

THE RELATION OF THE REFORMATION to all of the prior developments discussed in the Introduction is bewilderingly diverse. There are interpreters, particularly on the Catholic side, who contend that the reform was not so much a correction as a continuation of the abuses of the late Middle Ages. This is partly a matter of definition. If the disintegration of scholasticism and the theocracy was an abuse, then Protestantism was unquestionably a continuation. All would agree that moral laxity was an abuse. But even at this point there is diversity of interpretation among Catholics, some of whom say that Protestantism was in the line of succession, because instead of restoring discipline the reformers abolished the rules, substituting clerical marriage for clerical concubinage. Other Catholic historians regard Protestantism as an honest attempt to eradicate avarice and lust, but with such intemperate zeal as to issue in insubordination.

If the term "abuse" be dropped and the inquiry be directed simply to the relation of the Reformation to the late Middle Ages, the answer becomes no simpler; for Martin Luther, the inaugurator of the reform, was a figure like St. Augustine into whom all things flow and from whom all things go. One might use the figure of a bundle of vari-colored threads drawn through a ring and twisted in passing so that every thread emerges but the pattern is changed. That is why Augustine can be regarded both as the epitome of classical and Christian antiquity and as the precursor of the Middle Ages. Luther similarly may be considered a medieval figure ushering in the modern age.

His relation to all of the late medieval movements is one alike of affinity and change. The reform as it developed exhibited a parallel to the late medieval spawning of sects. But Luther's revolt did not arise from a sectarian interest. Only slowly was he driven to endorse certain opinions of the Bohemian sectary, John Hus, and sought always to curb the sectarian impulse within Protestantism. Nor did the reform take its departure from late scholasticism with its disparagement of philosophy and reason, though Luther always held that philosophy cannot scale the heights of faith. In some respects he remained a disciple of the scholastic, William of Occam. Yet to pass from the reading of Occam to Luther is to move through the same air from the Arctic to the Equator. The Reformation had indeed something in common with the Renaissance. Both movements decried pilgrimages, indulgences, the cult of relics and of the saints. But Luther lived to rail against Erasmus almost more than against the pope. Protestantism was not an accommodation of religion to nationalism. However much Luther as a German might berate the arrogance of the Italians, the Lutheran movement gained for a time a strong following in Italy. The reform aspired to win all Europe and in a measure succeeded. The Reformation was not primarily a revolt against economic exploitation, because although some might gain through the expropriation of ecclesiastical wealth, the leading reformers were churchmen who forfeited their livings in exchange for meager and pre-

carious stipends at best, and at worst for exile or death.
Neither was the movement in the first instance a prophetic
outcry against immorality. Luther had actually less to say
about current irregularities than a contemporary like Sebastian Brandt, who in rhyming couplets complained: "St.
Peter's bark is tempest-tossed. I fear the vessel may be lost."
A woodcut shows the saint on the bank trying with a huge
key to hook the boat and bring it to shore. The unworthy
crew are castigated.

Luther's initial cry was not a castigation of the crew. It
was the ship to which he objected. "Others," said he, "have
attacked the life. I attack the doctrine." Not the abuses of
medieval Catholicism, but Catholicism itself as an abuse of
the Gospel was the object of his onslaught. Luther congratu-
lated Erasmus for perceiving what others had missed, that
the quarrel centered on the view of man and God. The
Catholic Church had in his judgment too low an opinion of
the majesty and the holiness of God and too high an estimate of the worth and potentiality of man. And this was
true not of the worst Catholics, but of the best. Therefore
the greatest struggle of Protestantism with the Catholic
Church was to be not with the flippant popes of the Renaissance, but with the fanatical popes of the Counter Reformation.

The quarrel was basically religious because Martin Luther was above all else a man of religion. This is the place
at which to start if one would understand either Luther or
the Reformation. Many other factors were in time to enter,
as is bound to be the case with any movement which wins
widespread acclaim, but religion was the start. Luther was
reared on the fringes of Christendom near the Slavic border
in a region remote from the enervating and exhilarating

ST. PETER'S BARK

breezes of the Italian Renaissance. The northern forests were still the abode of Gothic man, straining through the tops of lofty trees for a glimpse of the illimitable. Luther had not been nurtured on Boccaccio and Aretino but on the *Sanctus* and the *Confiteor*. He had not been titillated by woodcuts of the dalliances of Aucassin and Nicolette, but rather terrified by depictions of Christ the Judge seated upon a rainbow with a lily protruding from one ear and a sword from the other, signifying mercy to the saved and wrath for the damned, who were to be consigned the one to eternal bliss, the other to torment everlasting. The best sellers of the period were not on *How to See Rome*, but on *How to Avoid Hell*.

The Church played alternately upon fear and hope that men might be neither too complacent nor too petrified to avail themselves of the means of grace. When hell was portrayed in such lurid colors as to instill despair, then purgatory was introduced by way of alleviation. Purgatory was a middle ground between hell and heaven, where the purgative process might be continued as a preparation for paradise. If this prospect then induced complacency, purgatory was stoked almost to the temperature of hell and in turn indulgences were introduced as a mitigation. Such oscillation between fear and hope was enough to engender conflicts in the souls of the sensitive, and Luther was inordinately sensitive. From his youth and throughout his life he was subject to acute depressions as well as to moments of high exaltation.

The prospect of the judgment day on occasion filled him with panic. His fear was all the greater because he believed in sinister spirits conspiring for his doom, the denizens of hell who roamed abroad and infested the earth, riding on the wings of the wind, lurking in woods and waters, ready ever with sardonic laughter to lure and bolt the unwary into hell.

Luther had been well instructed as to the measures which man can take to guard himself against the Prince of Darkness and insure the favor of the Prince of Light. He might receive most of the seven sacraments, he might perform the seven works of mercy, he might enlist the aid of twice or thrice seven heavenly intercessors. But nothing he could do would be so effective as to take the cowl. The monastery was the way par excellence to heaven, because the monastic life was shielded alike from the distractions and the complications of the world so that here one might pursue the contemplative life and practice the most meritorious virtues. The Church differentiated levels of moral achievement, some incumbent upon all and deserving of lesser reward, some reserved for the elite and meriting greater recompense. The ten commandments applied to all, but the injunctions of Jesus — to sell all, forsake father and mother, wife and child, resist not evil — being impractical or difficult of attainment in the world, were reserved for the cloister. The monk should have no goods, no wife, no weapons. Poverty, celibacy, and pacifism belong not to the commands but to the precepts of the Gospel. These were the counsels of perfection and these conferred an unusual reward. The monastic vow was regarded therefore as a second baptism washing away all intervening sins, and so efficacious was the cowl that those who had not taken it in life desired to wear it in death. Erasmus scoffed at the popular notions when he related the story of a Dominican who in a shipwreck discarded his cowl and naked plunged into the sea while calling upon the saints. How should they recognize him without his uniform?

Luther was in no mood to scoff when in his twenty-second
year on a sultry day of July in 1505 he was caught in a
violent thunderstorm and smitten by lightning to the ground.
In that sudden confrontation with death, he did what many
another medieval man had done; he cried, "St. Anne help
me, I will become a monk." The vow was unpremeditated
but not unprepared. He was a student of the law and a
master of arts at the University of Erfurt, planning on a civil
career in accord with the wish of his father that he should
prosper and support his parents in their age. But all the
ideas on which Luther had been reared, all the lessons which
he had imbibed in church and school had acquainted him
with the one sure recourse of the afflicted soul. He took the
most certain way and entered an Augustinian monastery.

The decision brought him only temporary surcease and
the old devastating fear recurred that because of his sins
he would be rejected by God, condemned by Christ, and
consigned forever to the arm of Satan. Luther was all the
more panic-stricken because he entertained so exalted and
so vivid a concept of God, the majestic, the all-holy, who
inhabits eternity, sits upon the circle of the earth, in whose
presence the angels bow, at whose nod the earth trembles,
whose ways are past finding out, whose judgments are ter-
rible, without whom there can be no security and with whom
so long as man is evil there can be no peace. Attracted and
repelled, exalted and devastated, Luther wrestled with the
Most High.

The Church offered many ways of bridging the gap between God the Holy and man the wrongdoer. The first is
the way of self-help. This was the point at which monasticism, as already indicated, afforded the greatest opportunity. As contrasted with life in the world, any form of

monasticism appeared more rigorous and worthy of reward. But Luther was soon to discover levels within monasticism itself. Even in the cloister one could jog along in a routine way or one could seek to take the kingdom of heaven by storm through extraordinary renunciations. In his youth Luther had seen on the streets of Magdeburg the emaciated figure of the Duke of Anhalt who had renounced his exalted position in the world to become a monk and had subjected himself to such severities that he appeared a walking death's head. Luther resolved to lay upon himself all of the austerities he could support. He engaged in long vigils, he fasted, he cast off all the garments that decency would permit. In after years he believed he had permanently impaired his health by such rigors. But never could he gain the assurance that even his utmost effort would avail to give him any standing in the eyes of God. The very best that he could do was in any case only what he ought to have done, and if he were able in a particular instance to fulfill God's commands he would not thereby have acquired any superfluous merit which could be transferred to the debit side of the ledger. Here lay the fundamental weakness of the penitential system. It was individualistic with regard to sins and virtues, assuming that specific offenses could be expiated by specific penances and that particular achievements beyond the level of ordinary attainment could be utilized to redress the balance. Luther came to the conclusion as a result of his own failures that sins cannot be treated singly because the very nature of man is so perverted that he needs to be drastically remade, and since no act, however meritorious, exceeds the demands of the occasion there can be no superfluous and transferable credit.

Luther came speedily to this conclusion as far as his own

deeds were concerned, but for some time he clung to the view that the saints had been so superior that their extra virtues constituted, as the Church held, a treasury of merit which could be rendered available by papal fiat through indulgences for the benefit of those whose accounts were in arrears. The shattering of this confidence is the primary significance of the trip which Luther made to Rome in 1511. He went simply on the business of the order but sought to avail himself of the unparalleled opportunities afforded at Rome to visit sacred shrines and to view sacred relics and in so doing to appropriate the merits of the saints. But although he climbed on his knees the sacred stairs of Pilate's judgment hall, believed to have been transferred from Jerusalem to Rome, and although each stair was kissed for good measure, at the top Luther straightened himself and ejaculated, "I wonder if it is so!"

But the Church has other means of salvation. Self-help is only one. Not the making of saints but the saving of sinners, who are vastly more numerous, occupies the Church's primary attention. The way of salvation for sinners is found in the sacraments, and the sacrament which above all others affords forgiveness of sins is penance. It consists of three parts, contrition, confession, and satisfaction. Luther had trouble with all three. Satisfaction was excluded at the outset because nobody can make adequate amends for sin. But this was not fatal because absolution is given after confession and prior to satisfaction. Luther's problem centered on contrition and confession. The Church to make things easier attenuated contrition to attrition, that is from genuine remorse to a mere regret arising from fear. Luther despised all such subterfuges, restored contrition to its full rigor and then was tormented to know whether he could satisfy the demand. How could anyone know whether his contrition was adequately drastic? And then there was confession. Open sins can readily be confessed, but how about secret sins, which are secret not only to the outsider but to the sinner himself? They elude his memory which is very conveniently co-operative with his self-esteem. They escape even his own recognition. So often man sins without compunction. Adam and Eve after the great disobedience went blithely for a walk in the cool of the day, and Jonah after fleeing from the divine commission went to sleep in the hold of the ship. Man does not even recognize himself as a sinner until confronted by an accuser. How then can anyone ever be certain that he has confessed everything? And if forgiveness is contingent upon confession and complete confession is impossible, what then? If man is so weak that he cannot bring forth fruits meet for repentance, what hope can he entertain?

The Church had another answer. It was the way of the mystic who without rejecting the penitential system yet pursued an essentially different course. Man, said the mystic, should cease his striving and yield himself to God. As the drop is merged in the ocean, so should the devotee sink himself in the abyss of the Godhead. The Christian mystics avoided the extinction of personality but they did posit so intimate a union of man with God as to speak of the deification of man. The English mystics used the term "to be godded." If this happens, then the weakness of man is overcome by the power of God. There is, however, one condition. Man must love God. This only is required of him, that he surrender in love. Then will all of his ego be restrained and everything contrary to God will be submerged. In the being of God he will delight himself and in the love of God he will taste eternal bliss.

Luther tried this way also but his picture of God and his picture of man made the mystic way impossible. In the first place, God is no abyss. He is infinite majesty, He is utter holiness, He is a consuming flame, and man, for all his weakness, is strong enough to be a rebel. He has broken God's laws and defied His majesty. Far from sinking himself in the ocean of the Godhead, man, like Adam, must hide himself in some recess of the garden.

And then a deeper and more devastating doubt assailed Luther's spirit. He could not love God because he suspected that God is not lovable. Man does not naturally love the unlovely, and God is unlovely if he is not even just, if he damns men without reference to their desert. Some of the late scholastics, on whose theology Luther had been reared, claimed that God is a law unto himself. He deigns to recognize merit only as it may please him. Man's fate is undetermined, and God's decision is capricious. No one can have any assurance of being saved. Then there was the Augustinian view, growing out of the theology of the founder of that monastic order to which Luther belonged, according to which man's fate is already predetermined, favorably or adversely, but man does not know in which way. Nothing that he can do will make any difference. The damned are damned, do what they will. The saved are saved, do what they may. God has made them so that they cannot do otherwise, and has disposed of them in advance according to his pleasure. What fairness is there in this? What justice? Is not a God who so acts to be considered base, cruel, despicable? Who can love such a God? "Love him?" said Luther. "I do not love him. I hate him."

Luther had spoken the word of blasphemy, the supreme sin, because directed against the highest of all beings, against the majesty of God. Luther's confessor endeavored to turn his thoughts to Christ, but this did not help because Luther conceived of Christ also as the judge sitting upon the rainbow, consigning the saved to heaven and the damned to hell.

Despair invaded Luther's spirit. Panic swept over him. He trembled at the rustling of a wind-blown leaf. Prayer afforded no surcease, for the tempter was always at hand insinuating doubts. Of what avail is prayer when addressed by man who is dust, ashes, and full of sin to a God who is holy, majestic, and devastating?

Luther took these questions to his confessor who endeavored to make available to him all that the Church had to offer by way of consolation, but to the deepest perplexities the confessor could only answer, "*Ich verstehe es nicht,*" — "I do not understand." But the confessor was a very wise man. He would divert Luther from morbid introspection by requiring of him activity for the sake of others. He should take a doctor's degree, become a preacher, and assume the chair of Biblical studies. Luther gasped. So much work would kill him. "Quite all right," was the answer, "God has plenty of work for clever men to do in heaven."

Luther began to conduct classes on the Bible. He was thus forced to wrestle with the source book of Christianity. One may wonder why so agonizingly earnest a spirit should not have thought earlier of this expedient. The only answer can be that he was following a prescribed course. Now that the Bible was given to him he gave himself to the Bible, and read it of course as a Christian book from end to end because the Church had long held that the pre-existent Christ was speaking through the patriarchs, the prophets, and the psalmist.

Luther's first lectures in 1513-15 were on the Psalms. He worked diligently and lectured on them, faithfully taking up the Psalms in numerical sequence. The study of the Twenty-second Psalm brought illumination. This Psalm begins with the words which Christ quoted upon the cross, "My God, my God, why hast Thou forsaken me?" Luther was suddenly arrested by that word *forsaken* as he had been by the lightning on that July afternoon. Christ forsaken! What could this mean? Forsaken, abandoned, alienated and estranged from God? That was precisely the way Luther felt. Christ had experienced all this too, but why? Luther knew why he felt forsaken. God is pure, man is impure. God is strong, man is weak. But Christ was not impure, Christ was not weak. Why then was he forsaken? The answer must be that he who was without sin for our sakes became sin and so identified himself with sinful humanity as to take unto himself the iniquity of us all, and to sense such a solidarity with mankind as to share in the estrangement from God. What a picture of Christ is this! The judge upon the rainbow has become the derelict upon the cross. He is still the judge and must be, so long as truth judges error and right judges wrong. But in the very act of judging the sinner he has made himself one with the sinner, assuming his punishment and sharing in his very guilt.

And what a new picture of God is here! Luther, as no one before him in more than a thousand years, sensed the import of the miracle of divine forgiveness. It is a miracle because there is no reason for it according to man's standards. That is why Luther so decried reason and by reason he meant the measure of man's mind. Forgiveness from the human point of view makes sense because man has need of forgiveness and ought for that reason to forgive. But God has no need of forgiveness. He is the all-holy and man having received from God naught but good has been ungrateful and rebellious. One would assume that God would consume man in his anger but it is not so, and that is the incredible wonder of the God revealed in Christ. "Of old," said Luther, "God came on Sinai with terror, but now in forgiveness. There He was to be feared in the midst of thunder and lightning. Now He comes with hymns of praise. Then He commanded that 'whoever should touch the mount should be put to death.' Now He proclaims 'Tell the daughter of Zion her king cometh unto her.' There His presence was announced by the sound of trumpets. Here He stands weeping over Jerusalem. Formerly the children of Israel fled before the voice of God. Now our longing to hear it cannot be stilled." The God of majesty is the God of compassion. The Lord of the hurricane is the Father who pitieth His children. All this we must believe and accept. Credence and trust, these only are required, for by faith and only by faith are we saved.

2

Luther's Reform

In reaching this conclusion Luther in no sense considered himself to be an innovator. The Apostle Paul had said the same thing in the Epistles to the Romans and the Galatians, and St. Augustine, the founder of Luther's order, had likewise excluded any contribution on the part of man to his salvation. But if Luther was merely reviving Paul the Apostle and Augustine the Doctor of the Catholic Church, one may wonder why there should have been any conflict with the Church. The answer is that Luther was really pitting one type of Catholicism against another, Augustinianism against Thomism. The difference is not great because St. Thomas also posited that in the end everything depends upon God, but he insisted that man through the power conferred upon him by God is able to contribute to his salvation. Luther, who is often reproached for a contempt of logic, was at this point rigorously logical. If everything depends upon God, then nothing is left over for man. The dilemma is an old one and more than once has recurred within Catholicism. Almost certainly Augustine himself would have been proclaimed a heretic had he lived and refused to submit to the subsequent modification of his system. The Church holds that whereas salvation is imperiled if anything depends on man, morality is imperiled if everything depends on God. The Church prefers to leave this logical dilemma to be resolved in the light of glory rather than, with Luther, to leave the mystery at the point of the justice of God.

The break began over a very practical matter. Indulgences, as we have seen, rested on the theory of the treasury of the merits of the saints and Luther denied that the saints had any merits. Indulgences were being used not only for the mitigation of penalties, including release from purgatory, but also for the forgiveness of sins. The theory on that point had not been definitively declared, but there were papal bulls which promised remission not only of penalty but also of guilt, and indulgences were being employed as a device for raising revenue. Strictly speaking they were not sold but given, yet the giving was precisely timed to coincide with contributions graded on the basis of ability to pay. The income thus derived was equally divided between the pope and the abbot, bishop or prince in whose domain the indulgences were conferred.

Luther's own prince, Frederick the Wise of Saxony, had been granted the privilege of an annual proclamation of indulgences on the eve of All Saints' Day. Twice during the year 1516 Luther protested against the practice because in his eyes indulgences were both deceptive and pernicious, resting on the false assumption of the extra credits of the saints, and certain to induce complacency rather than contrition. This first protest of Luther deserves to be recorded because it demonstrates that he was not motivated primarily by indignation against financial exploitation, since the revenues of this indulgence were used to support his own church and university.

The next year occurred a much more flagrant example in

which all the abuses reached their peak. Albert of Hohen-
zollern, not old enough to be a bishop at all but already
holding two bishoprics, was offered the archbishopric of
Mainz if he would himself pay the installation fee. He
inquired of the pope how much further he would have to
pay to secure a dispensation for transgressing so many of
the rules. Leo X asked 12,000 ducats for the twelve apostles.
Albert offered 7,000 for the seven deadly sins. They com-
promised on 10,000, presumably not for the ten commandments. Albert borrowed and paid the money. In order that
he might be reimbursed, the pope permitted the proclamation of an indulgence in his territories for the term of eight
years, half of the proceeds to go to Albert, the other half to
the construction of the basilica of St. Peter's. Albert in
his instructions to the vendors passed over his own share
in the transaction and instead bemoaned the deplorable state
of the bones of Peter and Paul, moldering in all weather
for lack of a covering. Let now generous contributions be
given to rear a mausoleum for the saints and a shrine of
all Christendom. Those who assisted were promised the
remission of all their sins, and, apart from any contrition
on their part, the release of their friends from purgatory the
minute the money clinked in the chest. Never before had
so many extravagant claims been combined.

On the eve of All Saints' in the year 1517, when the indulgences were again to be proclaimed in Wittenberg, Luther
posted on the door of the Castle Church ninety-five propositions for debate, popularly called the Ninety-five Theses, ·
directed this time not simply against the local practice
but against Albert's instructions. Not a word was said
about the sordid details behind the transaction. Luther
may have known nothing about them at the time, though

In filentio et spe erit fortitudo vestra.
Martinus Luther abconterfect.

Hanns Guldenmundt zu Nurmberg

MARTIN LUTHER

he could scarcely have been ignorant that Albert would receive half of the returns. But the theses were directed only against the instructions and the sermons of the vendor. Luther objected on three counts. The first was on the score of German national resentment against papal exploitation. In Luther's eyes this was the least consideration, but he made it and did so with characteristic vehemence. If the pope knew the poverty of the German people he would rather that St. Peter's lay in ashes than that it should be built out of the blood of his sheep. The second point questioned the jurisdiction of the pope over purgatory. If he could release souls why did he not empty the place? Luther contended, as did the more conservative theologians, that the pope could remit only penalties imposed by himself on earth. Indulgences do not affect purgatory and do not forgive sins. All of this had been said before and would be supported by many. The third point was of all the most devastating, as to Luther it was the most conclusive. Indulgences induce a wrong state of mind. The sinner who is primarily concerned to escape penalties is hopeless. He must be consumed with horror if he would be saved. God must kill before he can make alive. This is the pain of purgatory, and one should not seek to be released from it, for in this disturbance salvation begins. Peace comes only in the word of Christ through faith. He who does not have this is lost, though he be absolved a million times by the pope.

That word but few would understand. To Luther it was the crux of the case. The theses evoked an unexpected response, however, no doubt in part because they adduced so many considerations that among the diverse groups in Germany each found something to applaud. Not everyone grasped the point that the saints had no merits, though even the common folk did understand this to a surprising degree.

In the course of the ensuing controversy the pope at length clarified the teaching of the Church and repudiated many of the most blatant claims. He made clear that indulgences do not forgive sins but merely remit penalties. The pope has full power to remit those penalties which he has himself imposed on earth. In the case of purgatory he can only as a suppliant beseech God to make the transfer of merits. But even this more sober statement could never satisfy Luther because the concept of merit still remained.

The indulgence dispute speedily receded and came to be regarded as of minor importance because issues of vaster import were raised. Luther had the temerity, when the pope did not endorse his view, to deny the infallibility of the pope, and for good measure of a general council also. The pope had entrusted the refutation of Luther to a Dominican who asserted that: "The universal Church is virtually the Roman church which consists representatively in the cardinals, but virtually in the pope. Just as the universal Church cannot err on faith and morals, nor can a true council, neither can the Roman church nor the pope when speaking in his official capacity. Whoever does not accept the doctrine of the Roman church and of the Roman pontiff as the infallible rule of faith, from which the sacred Scripture derives strength and authority, is a heretic. And he who declares that in the matter of indulgences the Roman church cannot do what it actually does is a heretic."

Luther promptly replied: "You say that the Church consists representatively in the cardinals and virtually in the pope. I say that the Church consists virtually in Christ and representatively in a council. The pope can err, a council can err. If the Church consists virtually in the pope, what abominations will you not have to regard as the deeds of the Church? If the Church consists representatively in the cardinals, what do you make of a general council of the whole Church?"

Luther's reply was a categorical denial alike of papal and conciliar infallibility. He could not in consequence be branded forthwith as a heretic because the doctrine of papal infallibility was not formally promulgated until 1870, and there were still in the sixteenth century many like Erasmus who believed that the popes should be subject to the control of a council. At the same time conciliar authority was impugned by the popes themselves, who therefore could not condemn Luther solely for his criticism of councils. Debate was permitted and in the course of it Luther was made increasingly aware of the radicalism of his theological presuppositions. He was next driven to a repudiation of the authority of the Canon Law, the great legal code of Christendom. A medieval papal pronouncement on indulgences, clearly enunciating the treasury of the merits of the saints, had been incorporated within the Canon Law. Luther, when confronted with this document, sought at first to obviate the natural sense of the words, but on being pressed conceded the meaning and repudiated the authority. When later Luther consigned to the same bonfire the bull excommunicating himself and the Canon Law, the smoke of the latter was much more offensive in the nostrils of his contemporaries because another great bulwark of authority was demolished.

These attacks on authority were supported by an appropriation from the sectaries of the late Middle Ages of two devastating ideas: eschatology and predestination. Luther, like the sectaries, believed in the speedy advent

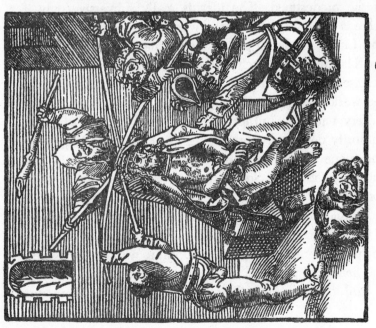

CHRIST AND ANTICHRIST

of Christ to overthrow his great enemy Antichrist, identified with the pope. There was this difference, however, between the view of Luther and that of his precursors. They equated particular popes with Antichrist because of their evil lives. Luther declared that even the most exemplary popes were Antichrist because the representatives of an institution opposed to Christ. The cartoonists of the Reformation were to take up the theme with avidity and in a series of couplets portrayed Christ born in the squalor of a manger, the pope elected in a military conclave; Christ so poor that he must find a shekel in a fish, the pope raking in revenues; Christ walking on foot, the pope borne aloft; Christ driving out money-changers, the pope reaping indulgences; Christ crowned with thorns, the pope with a tiara; Christ ascending to heaven, and the pope as Antichrist cast into hell.

The other idea was that the true Church consists only of the predestined. The idea is really subversive only if there is some way of knowing who the predestined may be, and Luther made no pretense of being able to tell, except for this, that the church of the predestined is bound to be despised and rejected of men, persecuted and hidden in the world.

Very naturally Luther was constantly asked, "By what authority dost thou these things? *Bist du allein klug?* Are you alone wise?" His answer was that he acted by the authority of Holy Scripture. He has been accused in consequence on the one hand of opening the floodgates of individualism, producing an inundation of all the vagaries of private interpretation, and on the other hand of investing one particular interpretation of Scripture with all the rigidity and finality of papalism. Both judgments contain a measure of truth if one looks at the outcome, because the Protestant sects did introduce a welter of interpretations and Lutheranism developed in the direction of stark Biblicism. Luther's own position was not precisely the one or the other. For him the ultimate authority was the word of God, by which he meant the self-disclosure of God through the incarnation, the crucifixion and the resurrection in Christ. This revelation was not restricted in time to the historical life of Jesus because the Christ is eternal and ever at work in the hearts of men, but the supreme manifestation was in the flesh. Of this stupendous event the Bible is the record. But although the record as such apart from the spirit will not produce faith, yet the Spirit does not operate apart from or beyond the record. Since the essential is the word uttered by God and not the letter traced by the scribe, different levels may be discovered within Scripture. In the New Testament Luther accorded the first place to the Gospel of John, then to the Pauline epistles and I Peter; after them came the three other gospels, and in a subordinate position Hebrews, James, Jude, and Revelation. James, though retained, was repugnant to Luther because of the insistence on good works, as was Revelation, because as Luther said, "It is not revealing." In the Old Testament also varying levels were discovered, with Genesis, Psalms, and Jonah rated highly and Esther disparaged as an example of Jewish vindictiveness. Luther treated Scripture with royal freedom but not at whim. There was a clear determinative principle that the word of God is the message of redemption through Christ Jesus our Lord without any merit on our part, and that we are saved solely through heartfelt acceptance in faith. Yet despite the recognition of levels within Scripture, Luther did treat the book as a whole and shrank from demolishing the canon by excluding James and Esther. The pope, the councils and the Canon Law might go, but to tamper with the traditional selection of the holy writings was one step too much. Necessarily, then, if the Bible was taken as a whole and yet not regarded as uniformly valuable, some portions had to be taken literally and others spiritualized. This is the point at which Luther often appears arbitrary and even inconsistent.

The drastic consequences of his position became apparent when he came to deal with the sacraments of the Church. Since the high Middle Ages the number had been set at seven: marriage, ordination, extreme unction, confirmation, penance, the Mass, and baptism. Luther's definition was that a sacrament must be an outward sign of an invisible grace instituted by Christ and exclusively Christian. By these tests he was constrained to reduce the number to two, namely the Lord's Supper and baptism.

Marriage is not a sacrament, he held, because it is universally valid not only among Christians but equally among non-Christians such as the Jews and the Turks. It was indeed instituted by God and approved by Christ and should be blessed by the Church. Luther had no mind to make it merely a civil contract, but it is not a sacrament in the strict sense of the term and for that reason is not a monopoly of the Church. This assertion undercut one of the devices whereby the Church in the Middle Ages had exercised control over lay life. Unions were prohibited up to the seventh degree of physical relationship and also on account of spiritual relationship incurred through standing sponsor at baptism. Except, however, in the case of close blood ties the prohibitions could be relaxed by the authority of the Church. Since the royal houses of Europe were interrelated, scarcely any marriage could be contracted without ecclesiastical investigation and dispensation for an appropriate fee. When then marriage was declared not to be a sacrament at all, the state stepped in where the Church went out and the prohibited degrees were dropped in the process.

Ordination was not a sacrament because not instituted by Christ. Ordination is a rite of the Church, but it confers no invisible grace and no indelible status. The minister is a Christian set apart by the congregation for the performance of a particular office. He is not thereby constituted a priest because all Christians are priests. Here was the doctrine of the universal priesthood of all believers. Merely in the interests of good order some are selected for the performance of particular functions. But if the difference between the clergy and the laity is so slight, the basis for a clerical theocracy is gone.

Extreme unction, that is anointing with oil when on the point of death, was in Luther's eyes mere superstition. Confirmation was retained as a rite of the Church, but not as a sacrament because not instituted by Christ. Penance might be considered a sort of half-sacrament because Christ did say, "Be penitent." And confession is useful if not institutionalized. Strictly speaking there are, however, only two sacraments, the Lord's Supper and baptism.

As to the nature of these two, Luther quite agreed with the Church that they are in no sense contingent upon the moral character of the celebrant. If he intends to perform the sacrament and if he uses the proper form, his personal unworthiness does not prevent him from being a ministrant of divine grace any more than the hypocrisy of a preacher can make the word of God to be a lie. But Luther insisted that faith on the part of the recipient is necessary. The sacraments do not operate in and of themselves *ex opere operato* in any magical way. Without faith there is indeed something there, but the recipient takes to his hurt rather than to his healing.

In the case of the Mass Luther was strongly insistent that there is no sacrifice. The priest does not offer up God upon the altar. Calvary is not re-enacted. The reason is that a sacrifice is something presented by a man to God, whereas man is simply incapable of offering anything. God gives, man receives and is thankful. The Supper of the Lord was originally called a eucharist, that is to say, a thanksgiving, and this is still its primary meaning. Luther denied the doctrine of transubstantiation, according to which when the priest pronounces the words "This is my body," the accidents of bread and wine remain but the substance is altered into the body and blood of God. Any such miracle performed by the word of man Luther repudiated, but he did not deny a real and even a physical presence. His position was that matter and spirit are not antithetical. The physical was created by God, is permeated by God, and is a fit vehicle for communication of the divine. God is omnipresent in all the material world, and Christ as God is also ubiquitous. But we do not perceive their presence because our eyes are holden. God is a hidden God who has chosen to make himself known at three points: in the flesh of Christ, in the word embedded in Scripture, and in the elements of the sacrament. What the minister does, then, is not to make God, but to lift the veil and disclose his presence. The sacrament is a rite of communion with God and Christ and of fellowship with believers. These two words sum up the whole, thanksgiving and fellowship. To describe this rite, the expression *Lord's Supper* is to be preferred to the word *Mass* which is nowhere to be discovered in the Bible.

THE LORD'S SUPPER

Both bread and wine are given to the laity. Luther preaches from the Word. On the right, the pope, monks, and cardinals are swallowed by a beast signifying hell

Baptism, the first of all the sacraments to be administered, has been reserved to be discussed last because Luther's theory presented peculiar difficulties. He insisted that the sacraments are without efficacy apart from faith, but he retained infant baptism. In what sense could this be said to rest on faith? There were among Luther's followers those who came to feel that his position logically pointed to adult baptism after the individual had arrived at an experience of conscious personal faith. But Luther himself distinguished two levels of faith. There is faith awake and faith asleep. Since faith in any case is a gift of God, why should not God confer it upon a child? Then again Luther shifted his ground and held that the child was sustained by the faith of the sponsor because children are from the outset participants in the life of the Christian community. The question of adult versus infant baptism has very far-reaching consequences for the theory of the Church, because adult baptism goes with the view that the Church is a gathering of all who have had an experience of regeneration, whereas infant baptism points to the Church comprising the entire community in a land where everyone born is also baptized. Here is the problem of the sect and the Church, of the small, select, voluntary conventicle over against the comprehensive institution coterminous with state and society. Luther had a difficult time making up his mind between these ideals and Protestantism subsequently split into churches and sects.

The position at which Luther had arrived very vitally affected the entire relationship of the Church to society. In the Middle Ages the Church, as we have seen, operated through three branches, the papacy, the parish clergy, and the monks. Luther had denied the infallibility of the pope. He had reduced the clergy from priests in a special sense to mere

ministers, and the monks he had abolished entirely. He
was slow in coming to this conclusion, and it was not indeed
until after he had been excommunicated that he abandoned
the cowl. The reason was partly biblical, that no warrant
could be discovered in the New Testament for lifelong vows
of poverty, chastity, and obedience. But even more the attack was a deduction from Luther's principle that man can
do nothing to save himself. Inasmuch as monasticism was
regarded as the area par excellence where man could perform works of supererogation, Luther was destroying the
prevailing motive for taking the cowl. The monasteries need
not for this reason have succumbed and indeed Luther had
no objection if unmarried persons desired to live in community and engage in some form of religious endeavor,
provided they did not suppose that they were thereby in-
gratiating themselves with God. As a matter of fact, subsequent to the Reformation Catholic monasticism has become
less a way of salvation and more a vocation for the achievement of particular tasks on earth. And as such it might have
survived in Protestantism, but it did not, probably because
there was still another reason, namely that Luther repudiated
the distinction beween the precepts and the counsels of
perfection. The entire Christian ethic, he held, is binding
upon everyone and not upon monks alone. As all are priests,
so all are monks, which in practice meant that none are
monks because the Gospel is best exemplified amid all of
the tasks of daily life in home and school, workshop and
farm. These are the callings rather than the monastic life.
The ethic of the Gospel, then, is not to be conserved by
segregation.

Luther in all these ways had wrecked the medieval pattern for the Christianizing of the world. The papal, clerical

theocracy was gone because the pope was not infallible, and the clergy were not spiritually superior or more competent than the laity. The monastic technique of keeping alive the higher righteousness amid a select community was likewise gone. Luther was therefore confronted anew with the problem of the Christianizing of the world. A prior question was the nature of the moral life and how far it is attainable even by Christians. Luther had so insisted that man is incapable of contributing to his salvation as to make easy the inference that moral effort is pointless. And there was the still more devastating affirmation that the higher reaches of the Christian ethic defy achievement; the counsels of perfection are binding upon all and attainable by none, because God commands the impossible. Furthermore the ideal is recessive. Every attainment raises the level of demand. The Christian life is a song not scored for breathing. After such devastation of ethics, Luther reconstituted morals by diverting attention from the achievement of tasks to the exemplification of the spirit. In two tracts of the year 1520, *The Freedom of the Christian Man* and *The Sermon on Good Works*, he declared that the Christian man is of all men the most free because he is not dominated by rules and does not pretend that he is carrying out laws. He is simply giving expression to his gratitude to God and to his love for his neighbor. The Christian man is of all men the most bound, but the obligation laid inescapably upon him is from within. The essence of Christian morality is the imitation of Christ, not in the medieval sense of doing just what Christ did but rather in behaving after the pattern of Christ, who, being rich, for our sakes became poor; who, being on an equality with God, for us took the form of a servant and a felon; being innocent, yet on our behalf he

assumed a guilt which was not his own. Even so must
the Christian become a Christ to his neighbor, so identifying
himself with the neighbor as even to assume guilt for which
there is no personal responsibility. This ideal also can
never be adequately attained. The Christian is bound every
day to fail, yet he is not sunk. He is at once a sinner and
yet saved. If he makes no pretense to goodness but in
humility and gratitude endeavors to conform himself to the
divine purpose, he will be able to carry on despite every
shortcoming.

As far as society is concerned the resultant view is one
of sober hopefulness. Luther envisaged neither a long
course for history nor the erection of a Utopia. Even Christians, he held, cannot restore Paradise, and the unredeemed
unless checked will produce a pigsty. But they can be
restrained, because even the natural man is not devoid of
moral insight and capacity. When Luther said that all men
are sinners he did not mean that all men are criminals.
In the eyes of God no man has any standing but from the
point of view of society he may be a good husband, father,
and magistrate. The Turkish Empire, said Luther, is better
administered than a Christian state. At this point he was
appropriating the Stoic Christian tradition of natural law,
according to which all men everywhere are endowed with
reason and able to recognize and administer justice when
their own personal claims are not involved. Therefore force
under law can be an instrument of equity.

It is to be exercised by the magistrate and by him alone,
for if force be used by each for himself anarchy is bound
to result. It is not to be wielded by the Church. Luther
excluded the sword from private and ecclesiastical hands.
He would countenance no revolution and no theocracy. The

state, he held, is the agency ordained of God to punish the
bad and protect the good. War, if justly waged, is a pursuit
in which a Christian man may engage, but only under the
constituted authorities and never on his own or under the
Church. The whole concept of a crusade as an ecclesiastical
enterprise was thus ruled out. The state within its own
sphere is to be unimpeded by the Church. Luther's ideal
was that parallelism of church and state which had been
espoused by the German emperors in the Middle Ages
against the papalists and had been eloquently defended by
Dante. It has never proved to be a workable plan. When
church and state are the co-ordinate arms of Christian society, one will prove to be the right arm and the other the
left. The outcome tends to be either Caesaropapism or
theocracy. Protestantism was to discover this all over again.
Lutheranism developed in the direction of Caesaropapism,
Calvinism developed theocracies, while the smaller sects
avoided both by a separation.

Luther's complete position was not matured in a day, but
his attack on indulgences was quite enough to evoke concern on the part of the papacy. There followed for a full
four years on the papal side a barrage of remonstrance,
threat, denunciation and fulmination, with interludes of
cajolery, negotiation and dilatoriness. The whole affair was
a disclosure of the degree to which the papacy had been
secularized. For a church with the presuppositions of the
Vatican, it would have been more honorable to dispose of
the heretic summarily than so to have dawdled. The reason
was political. The Vicar of Christ was also a temporal lord,
chary of alienating the German nation. The situation became all the more acute on the death of the Emperor Maxi-
milian in January, 1519. An election was thereby pending

and the electors were preponderantly German. The Holy Roman Empire was a somewhat amorphous legacy from the Middle Ages, once genuinely universal, now restricted by the encroachment of the new national states, but still so international that the heads of those states were eligible for the office of emperor. The rivalry in this instance was between France and Spain. The Germans desired neither because the emperor in that case would not be German; and the pope desired neither because either, if elected, would enjoy too great an accretion of power. The pope therefore made common cause with the Germans, and proposed as his candidate the elector Frederick the Wise of Saxony, who happened to be Luther's prince.

Frederick did not too well comprehend Luther but was concerned that a German subject should not be taken for trial outside of Germany, and should receive an impartial hearing. On the former count Frederick, unsolicited, early took steps to insure that Luther should be examined only on German soil. The first hearing was before Cardinal Cajetan at Augsburg in 1518, and the last before the Diet of Worms in 1521. The second stipulation was that he must not be condemned unheard, which was taken to mean that he must be convicted out of the Scriptures. But to determine whether or no this condition had been fulfilled was precisely the issue, and Frederick's own doubts on the point account for some vacillation. He could not of course control what the papacy might do, but he was resolved that the ban of the Empire should not be imposed unless the conditions were observed. Frederick's obstruction and the pope's temporizing protracted Luther's trial and gave him the opportunity to bring out the revolutionary manifestoes of the year 1520.

During this process all manner of ancient rivalries were re-aligned about his person. To begin with the Augustinians and the Dominicans were pitted against each other, the former as defenders, the latter as assailants. The Leipzig debate of 1519 drew in the rivalry between the two divisions of Saxony, the northern under the elector Frederick and the southern next to the Bohemian border under Duke George. The former became the great protagonist, the latter so much a bête noire for Luther that he could compose the trinity of opposition as "the Pope, the Devil, and Duke George." Then too the universities were arrayed, Wittenberg for the defense and Leipzig for the attack. The debate produced still another alignment. Luther was driven by his opponent to endorse certain propositions of the Bohemian heretic, John Hus, burned a century earlier at the Council of Constance. Since Bohemia thereafter had become not only heretical but crusading, and had invaded the territories of Duke George, no more invidious charge could have been fastened upon Luther than sympathy with such an enemy of the Church and land.

3

The Irreparable Breach

ALL GERMANY WAS BEING AROUSED, so much so that after the Leipzig debate Luther became both a national and an international figure. No doubt the publication of a collected edition of his Latin works at Basel contributed to his growing reputation.

The German nationalists rallied to his defense. This may well appear strange after his endorsement of the Czech, John Hus, but for the Germans the great enemy was not at Prague but at Rome, because Rome had done so much to disintegrate the Holy Roman Empire, an essentially German institution, and thereby had given the lead to France, Spain, and England in national consolidation. The nationalists therefore poured vitriol on Rome and offered Luther an asylum if his life were threatened. He was heartened by such proffered aid, but at the same time chary, for his was the cause of the Lord and should not rely unduly on the hand of man.

Luther became also an international figure through the support of the Renaissance humanists, who in those years saw rather the likenesses than the 'differences from Luther. The great Erasmus applauded much of what Luther was saying. The call to return to the simplicity of the New Testament, the scorn of scholastic subtlety, the invective against indulgences, against the veneration of relics, and against the cult of the saints fitted in perfectly with the humanist program. Luther's opponents were the enemies of sound learning, the breed of inquisitors who had hounded the humanists. Luther was hailed as *Eleutherius,* the free man. In the ensuing conflict Erasmus adopted a clear course. He would not endorse any more of what Luther was saying than he had himself already said. Indeed he feigned ignorance of Luther's views, while insisting that out of consideration for his upright life he should be given a fair hearing in a conciliatory spirit. But when Luther in the summer of 1520 came out with his tract entitled *The Babylonian Captivity,* in which he enunciated the view of the sacraments already described, Erasmus exclaimed, "The breach is irreparable!" At the same time for another ten years he sought to bridge it.

Pope Leo was at last made aware of the seriousness of the situation and bestirred himself sufficiently amid the pleasures of the chase to compose a bull appropriately beginning: "Arise, O Lord, and judge Thy cause. A wild boar has invaded Thy vineyard. Arise, O Peter, and consider the case of the Holy Roman Church, the mother of all churches, consecrated by thy blood. Arise, O Paul, who by thy teaching and death hast illumined and dost illumine the Church. Arise all ye saints, and the whole universal Church, whose interpretation of Scripture has been assailed." The bull gave Luther sixty days in which to make his submission, dating from the time when he received the summons. That was on 10 October, 1520. On 10 December, he celebrated the expiration of the respite by burning publicly the bull and the Canon Law.

Yet, because of political considerations, excommunication

did not immediately follow; and Frederick the Wise arranged
that Luther should have a hearing before the diet of the
German nation about to meet early in 1521 in the city of
Worms to confer with the newly elected Holy Roman Emperor Charles of Hapsburg, the King of Spain. The pope's
wishes as to the election had been defeated. Now his tactic
was to use Charles where he could and to embarrass him
where he could not. Frederick the Wise might still be
useful.

The hearing of Luther before the diet was an embarrass-
ment to the pope because it meant the examination of a
heretic by a lay tribunal. The procedure in the Middle
Ages had been that the secular arm without question executed the sentence of the Church. In this case, however,
there had as yet been no sentence out of fear for the German
nationalists. Curiously the Diet of Worms was turned into
a church council. Luther was tried by a lay court and
actually put under the ban of the Empire before being subjected to the excommunication of the Church.

At the diet there were three parties: the extreme papalists who desired that the diet or the emperor on his own
authority should implement the wish of the Church and
put Luther under the ban without discussion; secondly the
defenders of Luther headed by Frederick the Wise, who
was less committed to Luther's opinions than intent upon
fair play; and thirdly the Erasmians, who desired a settlement out of court by way of compromise. If only Luther
could be persuaded to repudiate the tract on *The Babylonian Captivity,* or at any rate to disclaim what he had
said about the sacraments, the other points could be negotiated, and alike schism and the warfare which might conceivably otherwise ensue could be averted. The German

nationalists were enlisted for the plan and Luther, while on the way to Worms, was invited to turn aside to a castle along the way there to confer with the representatives of the Catholic moderates. He replied that he would enter Worms though there were as many devils as tiles on the roofs.

On 17 April, 1521, Luther appeared before a small session of the diet. He was confronted with a pile of his books and asked whether he acknowledged them all, in the hope that he might repudiate *The Babylonian Captivity*. But Luther acknowledged every one of the books and added for good measure that he had written more. Then he was asked whether he would stand by everything which he had written therein. This was affording him another opportunity to discriminate and reject a part. Suddenly he became well-nigh speechless, as he considered the frightful responsibility which rested upon him in going counter to the teaching of the Church for so many centuries. Were his opponents justified when they inquired, "Are you alone right?" He asked for time. It was granted. In consequence he appeared the following day before a crowded session. Once more he was given an opportunity to repudiate a portion of his teaching. He responded by distinguishing three parts: the first having to do with Christian piety, which he could not repudiate without rejecting the Christian religion; the second having to do with German grievances which none in the diet would wish him to deny; and the third containing personal attacks which he could not well retract without giving too much comfort to the enemy. The examiner replied that he ought still further to have distinguished his works as those which were bad and those which were worse. Let him give an answer without horns: "Do you or do you not repudiate

your books and the errors which they contain?" **Luther**
answered, "Since Your Majesty and your lordships **desire**
a simple reply, I will answer without horns and **without**
teeth. Unless I am convicted by Scripture and plain **reason**
— I do not accept the authority of popes and councils, **for**
they have contradicted each other — my conscience is **cap-**
tive to the Word of God, I cannot and I will not **recant**
anything, for to go against conscience is neither right **nor**
safe. God help me. Amen."

Even after this unyielding reply an attempt was made **to**
break him down in a committee. He was reminded that **if**
he would not yield the outcome would be division, **insurrec-**
tion, and war. Luther's answer amounted to this, that **where-**
as in practical matters one may compromise, and even **as to**
principles may concede the possibility of error, never is **it**
right to deny belief in what one believes. "The pope," **said**
he, "is no judge of matters pertaining to God's word **and**
faith. But the Christian man must examine and judge **for**
himself." Here we have the epitome and the extent **of**
Protestant individualism.

Luther was thereupon placed under the ban, though **not**
yet under excommunication. For that reason the Edict **of**
Worms laid the stress upon his offenses against the **civil**
order, declaring him to be more of a menace to **political**
than ecclesiastical authority. Odd that this man, who in **our**
day is often considered subservient, was in his own **time**
adjudged to be subversive! Luther was given forty days **in**
which to return home. After the expiration anyone **might**
commit him to the authorities to be burned.

On the return journey Luther's party was attacked by **a**
company of horsemen and Luther was abducted. The **news**
spread throughout Germany that he had been assassinated.

But shortly his friends received letters "from the wilderness." He had been concealed by Frederick the Wise who instructed his chaplain to hide Luther without disclosing his whereabouts even to the elector, who would then be able truthfully to plead ignorance. Luther was in exile for a year at Frederick's castle called the Wartburg. This very retirement enabled Luther to lay the first foundations of the Evangelical Church. His literary productivity during those months was prodigious. He put out a collection of sermons which long served as a model for evangelical preachers. His greatest achievement was the translation of the entire New Testament from the original Greek into the German tongue. The Old Testament followed later.

Luther had an amazing felicity in language. His mastery of words was Shakespearean. Above all else he had a feeling unsurpassed for the subject matter. Luther could understand the cry of the Apostle Paul, "Oh miserable man that I am, who shall deliver me from the body of this death?" He had entered into the heights and depths of the penitential psalms, and could render the paeans because he knew the pangs. Words welled at times unbidden to his lips. On other occasions he had to labor, and to seek help for special terms, from the butcher in order to name the entrails of the sacrificial victims in the book of Leviticus, and from the jeweler for the gems of the new Jerusalem. "My aim," said he, "is to make Moses speak so that you would never know he was a Jew." Not only Moses but every character from Adam to John became German. The translation of the Bible is Luther's supreme religious and literary achievement. But it is a book sealed with seven seals save to his own people. A translation does not lend itself to translation. Faust can be turned into English and Hamlet into German

but the Bible must be taken afresh from the original into
every vernacular. Nevertheless one example may be ven-
tured of a literal rending of Luther's version. Take the
Twenty-third Psalm:

The Lord is my shepherd; naught shall I lack.
In green fields I am shepherded and led by fresh waters.
He quickens my soul, and for his name's sake leads me aright.
Though I wander in darkness, I fear no ill. Thou art beside
me. Thy rod and thy staff are my comfort.
Thou settest a table before me against mine enemies. My cup
is filled full.
Goodness and mercy shall go with me to the end of my days,
and I shall abide in the house of the Lord forever.

Luther was not to be permitted to solace himself in literary
labors. During his absence his followers in Wittenberg
proceeded to give concrete form to his ideas and thereby
brought the Reformation to the common man. Nothing
which Luther had done hitherto had made a practical change
for the ordinary Christian except the attack on indulgences,
and that had not yet taken effect because indulgences were
for a time still dispensed in Wittenberg itself. But much that
Luther had proposed demanded reformation of a concrete
character. The liturgy must be revised. He had declared
that the Mass is not a sacrifice, but the Canon of the Mass,
the core of the liturgy, declares that it is. The theory of
sacrifice was nowhere more prominent than in the masses
privately endowed and privately conducted for the benefit
of the departed. Twenty-five priests were assigned to the
celebration of such masses in the Castle Church at Wittenberg. Luther saw two offenses here: the first was the very
notion of sacrifice, and the second that the priest celebrated
alone without the fellowship of believers. Then too the

Hussite practice of giving the cup to the laity had received endorsement from the reformers. These changes, which Luther had advocated, his followers undertook to introduce.

Among the more prominent of his colleagues were Melanchthon, a young humanist professor of Greek at Wittenberg, and Carlstadt, an older professor who had conferred on Luther the doctor's degree. Carlstadt especially strode ahead, and on Christmas Day, 1521, summoned the city to a celebration of the Mass after the new fashion. Carlstadt officiated in plain clothes, omitted all reference to sacrifice in the liturgy, and used the German language for the words of institution. For the first time in their lives the congregation heard in their own tongue the words, "This is the cup of my blood of the new and eternal testimony, spirit and secret of the faith, shed for you for the remission of sins." Carlstadt invited the people to communicate in both kinds, that is to receive the wine as well as the bread, and allowed them to take the elements into their own hands. One man so trembled that he dropped the bread. Carlstadt told him to pick it up but he who had had the courage to receive into his own hand the sacred morsel, when he saw it desecrated on the floor, was so overcome by all the terror of sacrilege that he could not bring himself to touch it again. The majority overcame their awe. The new order had assumed the shape which the common man could see and taste. Luther approved.

The priests began to marry. Again Luther approved. Then monks deserted the cloisters in favor of wives. "Good heavens," exclaimed Luther, "monks too? They'll never give me a wife." He set himself, however, to examine the grounds for monasticism and came to the conclusion, as we have seen, that the system was devoid of Biblical warrant and inimical because primarily an effort to win heaven by self-help. In 1525 he sealed his convictions by himself marrying.

Thus far Luther endorsed the reforms which were being enacted in Wittenberg. Before long, however, the situation took a turn at which he was aghast. Violence broke out. The old believers were intimidated, priests were mocked, and dragged by their hair from the altars. However commendable the reforms, Luther could not condone such disorderly procedures. He had always held that the sword is committed to the magistrate alone and not to be exercised by the common man even in self-defense, and least of all in the support of the Gospel.

Even more was Luther outraged when such methods were used on behalf of reforms of which he did not approve. His colleague Carlstadt embraced one after another of the elements of a program anticipating English Puritanism. One of his underlying concepts was a dualism of flesh and spirit whereby the physical was construed as an impediment rather than an aid to the spirit. In consequence Carlstadt rejected images which minister through the eye, music which appeals through the ear, and the physical presence of Christ in the sacrament which mediates the divine through the mouth. The disparagement of the physical led also to simplicity and even austerity in dress and deportment. Carlstadt renounced all clerical garb and, though a minister, dressed in a great gray cloak as a peasant. A second principle re-enforced this position, namely social equalitarianism. The doctrine of the priesthood of all believers was taken so seriously that Carlstadt would not be called Doctor but only "Brother Andreas." The desire which also actuated Luther to restore the pattern of early Christianity was carried further to include many Old Testament practices. The destruction of images was based on the Mosaic injunction, as was also the introduction of a strict sabbatarianism. The entire program was alien to the spirit of Luther, who believed that the earth is the Lord's and the fullness thereof, and any portion may be used in the interests of religion. He saw no reason for carrying social leveling beyond the injunctions of the Apostle Paul, whose scheme of society was patriarchal. And any legalistic attitude to the Bible savored to Luther of a revival of Phariseeism. In order to cope with such tendencies Luther, at the invitation of the congregation and town council, returned to Wittenberg. Carlstadt was banished.

Such drastic treatment would scarcely have been meted out to him had he not been suspected, albeit without warrant, of collusion with a much more radical figure, Thomas Muentzer, whose major significance lies in the fathering of a new variety of theocracy. The ancient Jewish theocracy had been based mainly on soil and blood. An Israelite was less and less one who had personally sworn allegiance to the covenant with Jehovah and increasingly one who by circumcision in infancy had been made a member of the chosen people. The Catholic theocracy, however, was based on the sacraments. Muentzer introduced a new variety founded on personal predestination. The saints should rule the world. The idea may have come to him from the Hussites, for he lived on the border of Bohemia and may have imbibed from them the concept of the kingdom of the elect. Luther was precluded from taking any such road because he repudiated the whole notion of theocracy and looked, not to the saints, but to the citizens through their magistrates to restrain the evil propensities of man. Muentzer expected the saints to rule the ungodly.

The primary problem of course was to identify them. Luther believed that this could not be done, for although the elect will be persecuted one cannot infer that the persecuted are necessarily the elect, who are known only to God. The Hussites were not too far removed from the theocracy of ancient Israel, because Czech nationalism was an ingredient in their kingdom of the saints. Muentzer had a new way to identify the elect, who were to be recognized through an experience of conversion, the new birth in the spirit through the Holy Ghost. He was introducing an emotional test. Here was a theocracy based on piety, the most dynamic and the most disquieting of all foundations, because piety is fluctuating. Blood, soil and sacraments are tangible, but the spirit bloweth where it listeth. Muentzer's idea, even though no group recognized in him a father, was to prove a ferment and a torment in the history of Protestant theocracies. The essence of it was that those who have had an inner experience of regeneration should undertake to supply the tone to the community whether by example or constraint.

Muentzer was ready to use constraint. The imminent coming of the Lord should be hastened by placing now the sickle to the harvest, or to use a figure taken from the Apocalypse, the 144,000 should issue forth to the carnage of the ungodly. Muentzer found his following in the Peasants' War and that was why Luther was so enraged. In this instance were combined the two uses of the sword which he repudiated — namely, the sword in the hands of the citizen without magisterial office and the sword in the hands of a churchman, for Muentzer was a minister and unrolled the banner of rebellion in the very sanctuary. His capture and execution were to Luther the judgment of God.

When confronted by such radicalism Luther perceived at once his own relative conservatism. He would take the middle way between Rome and the firebrands, as he called them. But by repudiating the fanatics he did not conciliate the moderates in the Church of Rome who could not forgive him for rending the seamless robe through his return to Wittenberg and the establishment of an independent church. This was what Erasmus could not tolerate. For himself he needed the Church as an ultimate ground of authority because he lacked in himself any unshakable ground of assurance, and he cherished the Church also as the bulwark of the European unities. He would not be the Samson to push out the pillars of Christendom on account of trivial abuses. At length in 1524 Erasmus was persuaded to declare publicly and precisely what in Luther he found unacceptable, and he fastened on the doctrine of man. He claimed that man is not an inert block incapable of good or ill, but a creature endowed with freedom and able to contribute to his own salvation. There were two points here. The first was whether man is capable of doing anything at all, which Luther never denied. The second was whether what man does can affect his fate. Luther answered emphatically "no!" because man's destiny lies wholly in the hands of God, and salvation is vouchsafed only to those on whom he has conferred the gift of faith, and not all are so favored. Luther attributed the acceptance of some and the rejection of others to God's immutable decree and this admittedly was a rock of offense. Erasmus inquired why the anomalies of life should thus be projected into eternity and preferred to leave man insecure rather than to incriminate God. Luther answered, "God must be God."

Here is the point at which humanism and the Reformation

diverged. The one elevated man even though he might be lost. The other exalted God even though he might appear cruel. The recognition of this divergence did not, however, produce a clear-cut division of humanists and reformers. Some humanists, following Erasmus, stayed with or returned to Rome. Others like Melanchthon clung to Luther. And Erasmus and Melanchthon never ceased to correspond. Humanism became a wanderer between the camps. For the moment a more congenial hostel was to be found in the courts of Rome, until the Council of Trent. During the Enlightenment humanism invaded the Protestant citadels and among the sons of Luther Erasmus came into his own.

Even in the sixteenth century Erasmus had a Protestant following and curiously among the very sectaries who were smashing even the unities which Luther had left intact. In many respects Erasmus was much more subversive of medieval Catholicism than was Luther. There were three elements in Erasmus's position which the radicals could appropriate. The first was the way in which he envisaged the restoration of primitive Christianity. The central point for him was not, as for Luther, the doctrine of justification by faith, but the pattern of New Testament behavior, the exemplification of the Sermon on the Mount, the literal imitation of Christ. The second point was aversion to dogma, whether cold from Rome or hot from Wittenberg. Deeds are more important than creeds, and the amount of belief necessary for salvation cannot exceed the comprehension of the most obtuse. The third principle was inwardness, the spirit against the flesh and the spirit against the letter. The inferences drawn from this principle by Carlstadt have already been noted. Others went even beyond him and pitted the inner against the outer word, the spirit against the letter of Scripture, the illumination of the heart against parchment, paper, and the ink of the Bible. All of these deductions would have been anathema to Erasmus and yet in a sense he may be considered to have fathered them all.

Saxony in 1527 was in confusion. The land by that time had embraced the reform but every village had its own varieties. Several churches in the same community and even the same church on different occasions might have diverse forms of the liturgy. And the sectaries were insinuating their views. Some of the ministers were ex-priests who had acquiesced in the reform out of lethargy. The theological seminary at Wittenberg was not able to train a new clergy rapidly enough to replace them. The coalition of sectarian divisiveness and agrarian unrest menaced peace. Under the circumstances, how could any order be introduced and maintained? The Catholic bishops had remained with the old church. If superintendents were to be installed, by whom were they to be appointed? If the churches were to choose them, by whom should the churches be convened? Under the circumstances none appeared better situated and better qualified to take the lead than the princes of Saxony who had become increasingly favorable to the reform and could not be regarded as infidels befouling the sanctuary when they were risking not only their kingdoms but their lives by espousing the Lutheran gospel in defiance of the imperial decree. Luther at first did not wish to invoke the sword of princes against the sectaries. "Let the spirits fight it out," was his advice, because faith is a free gift of God and cannot be forced. Religious instruction, however, liturgical reform, and even a purge of the clergy might be instituted by the prince in the role of an emergency bishop. Such was Luther's view of the Visitation conducted in 1527 under the auspices of the prince. Unfortunately, however, what Luther countenanced as a provisional expedient hardened into a system, and even in 1527 the prince appears to have viewed the matter differently from Luther; the committee of clergy and laity appointed by the prince to "visit" the churches was referred to as "our authorized visitors" as if they were state officials. From this expression may be dated the beginning of the state church.

But Luther was certainly of no mind to leave to the princes the positive tasks of instructing and edifying the people. Both before and after 1527 he was busily providing new forms and materials consonant with the reform. First came the liturgy. Luther started simply with a revision of the Latin names with the excision of all references to the notion of sacrifice. But these changes proved to be inadequate because of the character of the congregation, which included not simply the ardent devotees of the reform but the whole community, among them many of the lukewarm. The question of the proper constituency of the church now had to be settled. Luther for a time experimented with the segregation of a nucleus of the fervent who should have some services apart from the merely formal Christians. But the attempt to form such cells proved too difficult, and by 1527 Luther had given up the plan. But if then the congregation consisted largely of the tepid and unenlightened, the service itself could not be simply an act of worship on the part of those already prepared, but would have to arouse and instruct. The liturgy then must be revised to include alike the praise of God and the teaching of the people. In 1526

Luther met the need by turning the service completely into German. The sermon was given a prominent place and the notices were often as long as the sermon.

The greatest innovation was congregational participation in song. Already in 1523 Luther had brought out a hymn-book. The words of twenty-three of the songs were from his pen and for some he is believed to have composed the music. At any rate he called in skilled composers and conferred with them, submitting to their judgment his own musical settings. In addition to the hymns, portions of the liturgy were versified and set to music to be sung by the entire congregation instead of chanted by the priest. No longer did the officiating minister repeat in Latin "I believe in God the Father Almighty," but the entire congregation sang "We all believe in one God only." No longer did the choi·intone *Sanctus, Sanctus, Sanctus,* but the whole assembly chanted a metrical version of the vision of the prophet Isaiah who saw the Lord high and lifted up and heard the cherubim and seraphim cry "Holy, Holy, Holy." Lutheranism became and remained democratic only in song.

In every possible way the people must be instructed. To this end Luther invited his assistants to produce a body of literature for the young. This is the first time in the history of the West that a "youth literature" was produced on any large scale. In the late Middle Ages the catechisms had been manuals to aid the priests in conducting examinations in the confessional. The humanists such as Erasmus had concerned themselves with the problem of education and the *Colloquies* of Erasmus and similar works began to supply the need of books to be read by the young themselves. The Reformation first filled the gap on an extensive scale. Before Luther's catechisms of 1529 five volumes of religious

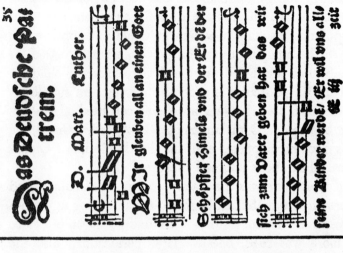

"We All Believe in One God Only"

booklets for children had been produced by his assistants for use in church and school. By 1529 Luther had come to feel that he must undertake the task himself for the reason that some of the radicals were using the catechetical method to popularize teaching of which he could not approve. In that year he brought out the Large Catechism intended for the untutored adult and the Small Catechism for children. The latter in particular is a gem, a ringing and simple affirmation of faith. The general scheme consisted of five sections: on the Ten Commandments, the Apostles' Creed, the Lord's Prayer, Baptism, and the Lord's Supper. Quaint Biblical illustrations adorned the text.

And then there was the tract. More pamphlets appeared in Germany from 1521 through 1524 than during any other four years of German history. This does not mean of course that more was read, because later periods had also the newspaper and the periodical, but for tract literature these years marked the peak. Most of it had to do with the religious controversy and not a little came from Luther's pen, but many others rallied to the cause. The printers shared in the labors and risks. The artists made of the woodcut an instrument of controversy. The Reformation was responsible for the cartoon. Simple, crude drawings showed Luther the German Hercules demolishing the Scholastics, or Lucifer breaking into Luther's study with a declaration of war because of the damage already done to his kingdom. The tracts were rough, often coarse, sometimes dull, usually uncommonly trenchant. They brought the reform to the common man.

The dissemination of the Lutheran movement created a political problem. Ever since the Diet of Worms Luther had been under the ban of church and state, but so long

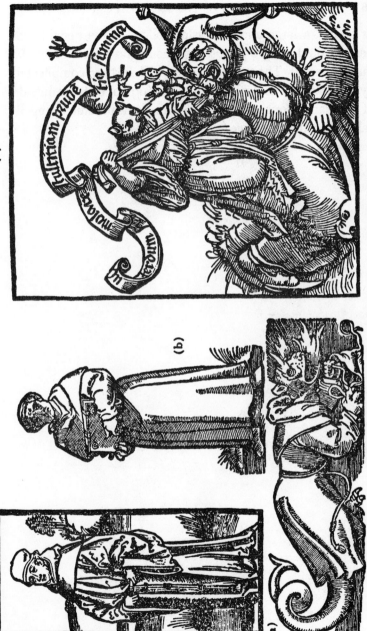

BLAST AND COUNTERBLAST (a) Thomas Murner—who really looked like this—was often portrayed with the head of a cat because his name was broken into the components *Mu-ner*. The second portion was equated with *Narr*, meaning fool, and the first with *Meouw*, the catcall. (b) Luther with the scripture astride the cat-headed Murner. (c) Murner's friends appropriated the taunt and showed him with the cat's head tying up the Lutheran fool.

as he had a large and increasing following the penalties of heresy could not be imposed without grave menace to the public peace. The situation was still further complicated by the accession to the ranks of the Reform of districts outside of Germany proper. Northern Switzerland became evangelical and to that area we now turn.

4

The Reformed Church: in German Switzerland

THE ACCESSION OF GERMAN SWITZERLAND to the Reform meant more than an accretion to the evangelical ranks. Here was a new variety of Protestantism, the precursor of many more until the prediction appeared to be abundantly fulfilled that one breach from the medieval unity would entail countless others, so that no middle ground could be found between allegiance to the one Church and an infinite proliferation of sects. Yet despite the variety this is not precisely what happened. The sects did not originate for the most part by a continuing process of separation. Neither was the number infinite. In many instances a new variety of the Reform arose independently for the simple reason that reform was so drastically needed. In certain cases there were offshoots from the parent stock, but in others more or less unrelated attempts were made to meet the same problem. Wittenberg, Zurich, Geneva, and Canterbury were sisters rather than lineal descendants. Nor were the varieties without limit. Only three or four main types emerged. The first was the Lutheran already described. It was marked by a profoundly religious sense, a deep assurance of overwhelming gratitude by reason of the mercy of God revealed in

Christ. The attitude to society was pessimistic. The kingdom of God cannot be erected on earth though villainy can be restrained, and the Christian should not withdraw but should lend a hand in the maintenance of order.

The two other main types differed from Lutheranism chiefly at the point of their positions with regard to the relation of church and society. The Reformed Churches of Germany and French Switzerland associated with the names of Zwingli and Calvin were more hopeful for the erection of the kingdom of God upon earth through the chosen of the Lord, the elect. The third type was that of the extreme sectaries, the Anabaptists, whose direct descendants today are the Mennonites and Hutterites and among whose spiritual children may be numbered the Quakers and to a degree also the Baptists and the Congregationalists. This group began at the point of the composition of the Church which should consist only of heartfelt believers and for that reason can never comprise the entire population of a district. Consequently the Church should not be united with the state, the more so because the Christianizing of the world is not to be expected. The Church then must maintain its purity and preserve its example by segregation.

A fourth type is perhaps to be set over against the others though it left but a slender memorial in the form of organization because its emphasis was upon a spirit of critical inquiry and an inward and often mystical faith. This movement of rational pietism affected in some measure all of the other groups and did find a recognizable concretion among the Schwenkfelders and the Socinians. The Church of England though an independent organization scarcely constituted a divergent type. In church-state relations and in the attitude to liturgy and music the affinities were with

ULRICH ZWINGLI

Lutheranism. The doctrine was frequently Calvinist though infiltrations from Renaissance Enlightenment were persistent.

The Reformation in German Switzerland may be dated from the year 1519 when Zwingli at Zurich commenced his reformatory preaching. He agreed with Luther in much. While minimizing his indebtedness he emphasized the agreement. On first hearing of Luther, Zwingli declared himself to be so much of the same mind that all he could learn from Luther was the courage to come out and say what he already believed. Luther appeared to him to be a stalwart champion of the same cause, and Zwingli undertook to disseminate Luther's German tracts by the hundred through colporteurs to every city, hamlet, congregation, and house in Switzerland. Zwingli agreed with Luther in the rejection of papal and conciliar authority, and in reliance solely on the word of Scriptures. Like Luther he preached justification by faith and denied the possibility of good works, the merits of the saints, and indulgences. With Luther he repudiated clerical celibacy and monasticism. With Luther he believed in predestination and in the reduction and revision of the sacraments, as well as in the simplification of the liturgy in the vernacular.

The common ground was large, but there were differences and in that age they were magnified. The first was that Zwingli by training and conviction was much more of a humanist and a disciple of Erasmus. In his Catholic period Zwingli had been a divided soul, a parish priest and a humanist scholar, with a divided parsonage, the bottom floor devoted to the cure of souls and the top floor to the pursuit of learning. He had a library of 350 works covering a wide range: geography, geometry, philosophy, religion, philology, and of course the classics in abundance. He was very much devoted to the humanists of his own day and especially to Erasmus, whose edition of the New Testament in Greek in 1516 filled him with such enthusiasm that he memorized the entire Pauline corpus in the original. By such study Zwingli was turned to the reform rather than by any agonizing struggle of the spirit of the sort through which Luther had passed. For that reason the emphases were different. Zwingli accepted the doctrine of rigorous predestination against Erasmus, but for essentially Erasmian reasons, because it was so clearly enunciated in the Apostle Paul rather than because for himself Zwingli had sensed the impotence of man. From Erasmus Zwingli took the emphasis on morals and the contrast of the spirit and the flesh, which was to lead him in several respects along the road already traversed by Carlstadt.

At another point Zwingli differed alike from Luther and Erasmus, and in this instance even more from Erasmus, namely in his Swiss patriotism. Erasmus was an internationalist, loath to concede that he was Dutch, scornful of Pope Julius II for bragging that he was a Ligurian Italian. Luther was very different in his address to his beloved Germans, but even Luther took good care not to confuse the Gospel with the fatherland. Zwingli was not so careful.

He had been a chaplain with the Swiss troops in the Italian campaign when they served as mercenaries for the pope. Switzerland was just becoming a European power because her sons in the service of other states had acquired the reputation of invincibility. In fact, when Francis I did once defeat them, so noteworthy in his eyes was the achievement that he had a medal struck on the field of battle commemorating the exploit. The popes, particularly because they had so few subjects of their own to conscript, turned to the Swiss and gladly availed themselves of the services of the Alpine hornets described as "the people of God to punish the enemies of the Bride of Christ." Zwingli soon came to be disillusioned with regard to mercenary service. Out of the 1600 men from his parish who crossed the Alps, one quarter were left behind on the plains of Lombardy, and Zwingli as the priest had to break the news to the widows. Others among the mercenaries returned, broken in body, enriched in coin, and corrupted in morals. Zwingli began to inveigh against all mercenary service whether for or against the pope or the French. This was his first appearance in the role of the reformer. One observes that he was crying out against a moral abuse, but his disillusionment at this point did not make him any the less disposed to use military power for either his country or his faith. On the latter score obviously he differed from Luther, who saw in him at this point a resurgence of the spirit of Thomas Muentzer.

A brief survey of Zwingli's reformatory activity will show how his principles were worked out. In the year 1519 he commenced his ministry in the Cathedral Church at Zurich. His reform commenced less as a protest than as an innovation, or as he would have said a restoration. He announced that henceforth he would no longer restrict himself to the prescribed biblical passages selected to be read for each Sunday of the year, but instead would preach on the entire gospel of Matthew from cover to cover with the Greek text in front of him upon the pulpit. The modern generation can scarcely reconstruct the excitement which such an announcement produced. A young humanist was in Zwingli's audience, Thomas Platter by name, who has left us a most

charming autobiography. So great was his ardor for the
ancient tongues that he supported himself through manual
labor by day and at night studied with sand in his mouth,
that the gritting against his teeth might keep him awake.
This lad, so passionately eager to master the wisdom of
the ages, when he heard from the pulpit the complete, un-
adulterated Word of God, for so many centuries withheld
from the people, declared that he felt as if he were being
pulled up by the hair of his head. The news of the discovery
of America had produced no such excitement.

Practical deductions were speedily made from biblical
preaching. Certain customs of the contemporary church
were declared to have no warrant in Scripture, three in
particular: the veneration of images, fasting during Lent,
and the celibacy of the clergy. These were all external matters which Luther always regarded as relatively unimportant.
Celibacy he abolished in the end and the food laws were
abrogated, but the images were retained and violent destruction severely condemned. The Reformation in the Swiss
cities by way of contrast not uncommonly began by the
eating of meat in Lent. That was the point in Zurich. Christopher Froschauer the printer declared that he had to have
meat to give him enough strength to bring out the New
Testament in Swiss-German by Easter. The offenders were
examined by the Town Council. The records contain this
entry:

. . . (c). Bartholomew Pur, the baker, said: On Ash Wednes-
day he and Master Uolrich [Zwingli], people's priest at the
Great Minster, Master Leo Jud, people's priest at Einsiedeln,
Master Laurence [Keller], parson of Egg, Henry Aberli, Michael
Hirt the baker, Conrad Escher, were in the kitchen of the printer's
[Froschauer's] house: and the printer produced two dried sau-

sages. They cut them up and each had a little bit. All ate of them, except Master Uolrich Zwingli, people's priest at the Great Minster. . . .

Though Zwingli himself did not eat, he justified publicly those who had done so. There came to be fighting in the streets, one man reproaching another that in his old cow country there was more concern for cheese and whey than for Scripture. Popular iconoclasm likewise commenced. That young Platter, who had been so exhilarated by Zwingli's preaching, stole a wooden image of St. John from the church, and when a caller came shoved the saint into the stove. The paint began to crackle. "Keep still, Johnny," muttered Platter. Priests began to marry. Zwingli joined with others in a petition to the Bishop of Constance requesting permission to marry in order to ease a guilty conscience. Clerical concubinage was a prevalent system in the Diocese of Constance, and when Zwingli judged that out of one hundred, nay, one thousand priests, monks, and nuns scarcely a single one was chaste, a canon of the church deprecated such open accusations but wished that they were not true. Zwingli when he came to Zurich frankly confessed that he had offended himself.

All of these questions were referred to the Bishop of Constance, and he in turn dealt with the Town Council of Zurich. This was not a case of a man against the pope but of a town against the bishop. The pope was singularly loath to estrange the Swiss on account of the mercenary service. Hence it was the Bishop of Constance who bore the brunt. Later when Zwingli persuaded the Zurichers to repudiate their alliance with the pope the case was altered.

Each of the innovations introduced at Zurich was first debated and decided by the Rath, a representative assembly of the town. The situation thus differed from that of Luther who had to deal not only with the city fathers but also with the elector of Saxony. In Switzerland there was no territorial prince and the government was by a local aristocracy. Under these circumstances the union of church and state in Zurich developed a much closer approximation to popular will than in Germany.

Three great disputations were conducted in Zurich to examine the questions which Zwingli had raised. Other points too were soon included: not only images, relics, food laws, and clerical marriage, but above all the Mass and the use of organs in the church services.

At the first of these disputations the Bishop of Constance sent a representative as an observer, not as a participant. Zwingli stood at a table on which lay the Bible in Latin, Greek, and Hebrew. The burgomaster called the meeting to order and invited anyone to accuse Zwingli. The bishop's emissary arose to say that he was not there to debate. Ancient usage ought not to be given up without a general council. "Who knows what France, Spain, and Italy may think about it? In the New Testament a general council is recorded in the fifteenth chapter of the Book of Acts. Ought not the universities to be consulted, Louvain, Paris, and so forth?"

"Yes," broke in Zwingli, "and Erfurt and Wittenberg." No other judge was needed, declared Zwingli, than the one before them on the table in Latin, Greek, and Hebrew. The teaching of the reformers, he insisted, was not a departure from ancient custom but rather a return to the most primitive custom of all. "But what are these new doctrines? The gospel? Why that is 1522 years old. The teaching of the apostles? Why, they are almost as old as the gospel. . . .

We will try everything by the touchstone of the gospel and the fire of Paul." In other words, the reformers were the restorers and the old Church was the innovator.

Someone then in the audience jumped up and demanded to know why the Bishop of Constance kept in prison a married priest if there were no biblical basis for the celibacy of the clergy. The bishop's representative was ensnared by this jibe into a reply and retorted that he had himself confounded that priest out of Holy Writ. Zwingli demanded chapter and verse. The bishop's delegate shifted to the authority of popes and councils. The verdict of the burgomaster was that he had been unable to produce the pike with which he stuck that priest. The Rath decided in Zwingli's favor.

The outcome of the three disputations was the abolition of the Mass in Zurich, the interment of the relics of the saints, the removal of images, the smashing of the organ in the cathedral, permission to eat meat in Lent, permission for priests to marry — of which Zwingli availed himself. Here plainly was a reformation much more puritan than that of Luther, who rightly sensed a similarity between Zwingli and Carlstadt. It became all the more evident when Zwingli rejected the real presence of Christ in the sacrament. Once again the three points were associated: no images, no music, no physical partaking of God, who must be worshiped only in spirit. Zwingli was a direct precursor of the English Puritans who maintained close contacts with Zurich.

As the Catholic practices were abolished new forms were constructed to take their place. The church service lost almost entirely its liturgical character and became well-nigh exclusively an exposition of the Word of God. First the Scripture was to be read in Latin from the Vulgate, then for

HÆc dicit dominus de⁹.

Sic dicit Papa⁹

CATHOLIC AND EVANGELICAL DEVOTION

On the left: "Thus saith the Lord." Searching of Scripture.
On the right: "Thus saith the Pope." Telling of beads.

the Old Testament the passage should be read also in Hebrew and the differences noted, then the Septuagint, the ancient Greek version, should be compared. The interpretations of the early fathers were adduced, then came the sermon pointing out the cohesion of the biblical passage, its force, majesty, eloquence, its use and fruit for piety, sanctification, justice, and constancy. But the people did not go to church, and the Council came out with a mandate forbidding any further loitering at sermontime on bridges, moats, and alleys. Lest any should fraudulently claim attendance at another church, the services in all three were placed at the same hour. One wonders whether as many persons do not go to church today as ever wanted to.

These changes had all been enacted by the Town Council and Zwingli's own position came to depend on the Council by which he allowed himself to be reappointed, seeing that his commission from the bishop had lapsed. Here was a union of church and state even more intimate than in Saxony with the difference that the state was more democratically constituted.

But other differences were more fundamental and were to make of Zurich a theocratic community resembling that of ancient Israel, resting to a degree on blood and soil. The first point, as in all of the Protestant theocracies, was the doctrine of predestination. The elect are the chosen people. And then of course came the question as to the elect. Zwingli did not despair like Luther of their identification, but he did not with Muentzer find the test in an emotional experience. The test was, rather simply, faith. This criterion serves better to include than to exclude. One cannot be certain that those who are for the moment without faith may not subsequently receive it, but one can be reasonably confident that those possessed of faith constitute the chosen.

The anomaly is that Zwingli was willing to equate them approximately with the population of Zurich, even with those who were constrained to go to church. Catholics of course were excluded. They might remain in the city but could not share in the government. But all of the inhabitants who subscribed nominally to the reform were included. Here was a very genuine problem. Zwingli had been inclined at first to construe faith in very personal terms. Had he followed this lead he would undoubtedly have been forced to segregate the true Church from the total community. But the pressures within and without brought him in a very few years to the point where he was ready to think of the whole town of Zurich, save for a few Catholics, as the elect company of the Lord.

He could the more readily do so because of his nationalism and his humanism. A strong Swiss feeling may well have helped the equation of the elect with the populace of a Swiss town and the Erasmian disparagement of externals led him to dissociate the sacraments from personal faith and to make of them rather the signs of membership in a community, comparable to certain rites in Judaism which made one a child of Israel. First for Zwingli came baptism. He made no pretense that it rests on faith. Precisely because baptism meant so little was Zwingli willing to administer it to children. To his mind baptism was nothing more than an initiation into a society, comparable to circumcision in the Old Testament. Similarly the Lord's Supper was separated from faith. According to Zwingli it is in no sense a channel of grace but only a sign and a memorial. It does less for the recipient than for the onlooker, because it is the public testimonial of adherence to a religious community. The Lord's Supper was likewise linked to the Old Testament and compared to the Passover, the memorial of the deliverance of Israel from Pharaoh. These comparisons were more than superficial. Just as circumcision and the observance of the Passover made the Jew a member of a national community, so baptism and the Lord's Supper marked the Christian as a member of a religious society. The Church then could properly be described as the new Israel of God, and since the pure Church in all details was discoverable only at Zurich, here at any rate was the spearhead of a theocracy. The test of predestination was faith, but faith was so far diluted that it could be made coterminous with a Swiss town. There was danger that the elect would become the elite.

From this they were spared by the precariousness of their position. The dangers were such that those who stayed in Zurich were as a matter of fact those who were prepared to suffer for their convictions. A theocracy is aggressive, and aggressiveness invites opposition. The first manifestation of the aggressive spirit on the part of Zurich was in the dissemination of the faith by missionary activity, which to the north met with success. Bern went Protestant and Basel went Protestant; Schaffhausen and St. Gall likewise, and the free imperial city of Constance. But to the south propaganda was unavailing. The ancient core of the Swiss Confederation, consisting of the forest cantons: Uri, Schwyz, Unterwalden, Luzerne, and Zug — these were solid for the old faith. Friction and violence arose in the boundary lands between Catholics and the Reformed. The Catholics caught and burned a Zurich image-breaker. The Reformed captured and executed a Catholic persecutor. The Catholics saw war in the offing and countered by making a military alliance with the traditional enemy of the Swiss, the House of Hapsburg. The troops of the Reformed then set out against the Catholic bloc.

But on the very field of battle the sentiment of Swiss national unity asserted itself and the troops made peace. One side brought a tub of milk, the other bread, and the confederates sealed their reconciliation in a common meal. The treaty with Austria was ripped by swords in public view, and the Reformed supposed that this First Peace of Kappel in 1529 had secured for them the right to preach

in Catholic lands. But whatever the understanding, such
was not the outcome. Protestant missionaries were still impeded, and even though the parchment of the Austrian treaty
was in shreds, signs were evident that the secret treaty still
held. Zwingli saw that alliance must be met with alliance.
If the Catholics turned to the Hapsburgs, the Protestants
would turn to the German Lutherans.

Their situation in the meantime had been strengthened by
the adhesion of new territory and a new spirit. Philip of
Hesse had been converted. He was young, energetic, politi-
cal-minded, and so eager to testify to his evangelical faith
that at the Diet of Speyer in 1526 he ate of an ox on a Friday.
The Lutherans, too, were menaced by threats from the
emperor and the House of Hapsburg, and Philip was quest-
ing for all possible help. An alliance with the Swiss would
be mutually advantageous but the theologians on neither
side would bless a military covenant unless there were first
agreement in religion. The Swiss felt that the Lutherans
were still tainted with popery. Luther by retaining the
doctrine of the real physical presence of the body and blood
of Christ in the sacrament had one foot still in Babylon,
and how would it be possible to wage a crusade against the
minions of Antichrist in alliance with a hybrid of hell? The
Lutherans in turn believed that the Swiss were of one stripe
with the sectaries, those emissaries of Satan, Carlstadt and
Muentzer. And how would it be possible to take the sword
for the reform of Christendom if a league had been sworn
with the disrupters of Christendom?

But for that matter, should Christendom be reformed or
defended by the sword? Grave searching of heart disturbed
the Lutherans on this score. Luther had long held that
the common man under no circumstances should take the

sword into his own hands. Above all, the sword should never be used in the defense of religion because the sword belongs only to the magistrate to keep the peace. If the Church is attacked she must suffer until vindicated by the hand of the Lord. Was that principle now to be abandoned at the behest of Philip of Hesse and in favor of the Swiss? Would it be wise under such circumstances so much as to meet with the Swiss and discuss theology at all? On the other hand, should theological agreement, if it were possible, be declined for fear of the political uses to which it might be put? The theologians agreed to meet.

The conference was held in the capital city of Philip of Hesse, at Marburg, in the fall of the year 1529. A truly surprising measure of agreement was attained. On only one point was accord impossible, and that was the Supper of the Lord. The great rite of Christian love had become the ground of contention. Yet even here more agreement was discovered than either side had expected. Luther insisted on the physical presence of Christ in the sacrament but agreed that whatever its nature the sacrament is of no value to the recipient apart from faith, so that any magical operation is excluded, and Zwingli agreed that the celebration is something more than a memorial because there is a spiritual communion with Christ. With this measure of agreement the Lutherans proposed a formula of concord which the Swiss rejected because it did not explicitly state that the presence is spiritual only. At the same time the Swiss urged that they should cherish each other as Christian brothers, and practice intercommunion. Luther was momentarily ready to accede until Melanchthon impressed upon him that a union with the left would close the door to the right and preclude any hope of reconciliation with the Catholics. The

conference ended without agreement, and of course no military alliance resulted.

Zwingli and his fellow Swiss went home to confront the Catholic cantons. Zwingli was still convinced that war alone could give the answer and that the Reformed should choose the time and place. But the Bernese were reluctant to commence open hostilities. Instead economic sanctions were applied against the Catholics who were deprived of wheat, salt and wine. Whereupon the old believers took the field. Eight thousand men advanced on Zurich, which could muster on short notice only some fifteen hundred who went out to hold the approaches until reinforcements could arrive. Zwingli and the ministers accompanied the troops. Zwingli went not merely as a chaplain but as a participant with helmet and sword. Here was the crusader, the priest in arms, the leader of an elect people, like Gideon of Israel, Ziska of the Hussites, or Cromwell of the Ironsides. The second battle of Kappel left on the field five hundred of the men of Zurich, and among them twenty-six members of the Town Council and twenty-five of the pastors, including Ulrich Zwingli. He was treated as a traitor and a heretic, his body quartered by the executioner and the ashes given to the wind. Luther did not soften at the news but regarded Zwingli's death as a judgment for having taken the sword on behalf of the gospel.

The treaty of peace which followed did not exterminate the Reform in Switzerland. Where already established it was left. The Catholic minorities were not to be disturbed in Protestant lands, whereas Protestant minorities were not to be tolerated in Catholic lands. The Reform might diminish, it must not spread. That it was permitted at all is witness to the triumph of the principle of territorialism. The Swiss Federation henceforth would be marked by two religions. The medieval unity of one God, one faith, one baptism in one country was gone. Switzerland offered a foretaste of the fate of Europe.

5

The Church Withdrawn:
Anabaptism

THE REFORMED CHURCH was to find its most influential em-
bodiment in French Switzerland under Calvin at Geneva.
But his movement can better be understood if first attention
be given to the emergence of the third type in the Anabaptists. Their movement arose in Zwingli's own circle as the
result of an effort to carry through more consistently the
program of the restoration of primitive Christianity. The
word Reformation is usually referred to the Lutheran movement, the word Reformed to the Zwinglian and Calvinist.
The word "restored" would be the most appropriate to apply
to those who by opponents were called Anabaptists. Their
great word was "Restitution." Much more drastically than
any of their contemporaries they searched the Scriptures in
order to recover the pattern of the early church.

What struck them was that the primitive church had been
composed only of heartfelt believers and so far from being
united with the state was rather persecuted, despised and
rejected, a church of martyrs. So always, said the Anabaptists, must the true Church be reviled, rejected, and crushed.
To this the Catholics and equally the Lutherans and Zwinglians replied that of course the Church was persecuted
in an age when the government was hostile, but after the

conversion of the emperor why should hostility continue? The state had become Christian and the Church could affiliate with the state and embrace the community. The Anabaptists retorted that the formal conversion of the emperor did not Christianize the state. The world remains the world, and if Christians are well spoken of, the explanation can only be that they have abandoned their witness. In the words of an Anabaptist hymn writer:

> "Yes," says the world, "there is no need
> That I with Christ should languish.
> He died for me and by his deed
> He saved me from this anguish.
> He paid for me, this faith can see.
> Naught else need be." . . .
>
> O brother mine, it is not so fine.
> The devil said this to thee.

The Anabaptist view rested upon pessimism with regard to the world and optimism with regard to the Church. The world — that is, society at large — will always be the partner of the flesh and the devil, but the Church must walk another road and must exemplify within her fellowship the living and the dying of the Lord Jesus. She must be a community of the saints whose members, though not perfect, yet aspire to perfection and strive mightily. The complaint against the Lutherans and the Zwinglians was that they had not produced a sufficient improvement in life. Promptly came the retort that the Anabaptists were reverting to monasticism and seeking again to win heaven by their good deeds, to which the answer was that they were not seeking to fulfill the law in order to be saved but rather to give proof of their faith by exhibiting its fruits. The kernel of Anabaptism

was an ethical urge. If the Catholic Church had improved
its morals they might not have found it too hard to return
to her fold, whereas Luther said that his objection to the
Catholic Church centered not on the life but on the teaching.

The Anabaptists called for a strict morality, and there
can be no question that they achieved it. The testimony
of their opponents is eloquent. Zwingli said of them, "At
first contact their conduct appears irreproachable, pious,
unassuming, attractive. . . . Even those who are inclined
to be critical will say that their lives are excellent." Zwingli's
successor, Bullinger, said that they denounced covetousness,
pride, profanity, the lewd conversation and immorality of
the world, drinking, and gluttony. A Catholic observed in
them "no lying, deception, swearing, strife, harsh language,
no intemperate eating and drinking, no outward personal
display, but rather humility, patience, uprightness, meek
ness, honesty, temperance, straightforwardness in such
measure that one would suppose they had the Holy Spirit
of God."

One notes in these testimonies the witness to their sobriety.
The movement for total abstinence from alcoholic beverages
stems from these groups. Not even Catholic monasticism
had called for total abstinence. Luther most assuredly did
not, but neither did Calvin or Knox. The Anabaptists moved
in this direction.

But if they were so exemplary why did the theocracy of
Zurich in the year 1525, with the full approval of Ulrich
Zwingli, pronounce against them the death penalty by
drowning? Why was Felix Manx, one of the first leaders,
sunk in the lake? Why was the old law of the Code of
Justinian revived, which visited death upon those who repeated baptism and upon those who denied the Trinity?

The Anabaptists did insist on adult baptism only, but was that enough to outweigh their Christian living and a warrant for exterminating them like superfluous puppies? That ancient law of Justinian, by the way, had been directed against the Donatists, a group who in the days of St. Augustine had endeavored to establish a church of the saints and had baptized over again any Catholics who joined their ranks. Yet this practice was not the real reason for the action against the Donatists, but rather that some of their number were disturbers of the civil peace. Unfortunately the offense specified in the law was not the breach of the peace but the divergence in the faith. And now in Zurich that superannuated enactment was revived in order to counter the Anabaptist attack on the Establishment.

The parallel between the Anabaptists and Donatists was, however, more than superficial. The first Anabaptists, to be sure, were not disturbing the peace but they did upset the whole structure of the Church, state, and society. Their theory of the Church made of it a conventicle and not a church of the community. Christianity, they said, demands a quality of living which can be and will be achieved only by heartfelt Christians who have truly died with Christ to sin and risen with him to newness of life. One cannot expect persons, merely because they have been dipped in infancy, to show forth the excellency that was in Christ Jesus, and baptism ought not to be given to babies because it is not a sign of membership in a Christian society, not a rite of initiation, but a visible token of that inward regeneration which has already taken place. In baptism, declared the Apostle Paul, we die and rise with Christ and this experience cannot come at birth, but only through an adult conversion and commitment. Those alone who have had this experience constitute the Church and all others would still belong in the world even though an ocean of water had been poured over them. Infant baptism consequently is no baptism at all, but only "a dipping in the Romish bath." To call these people Anabaptists, that is re-baptizers, was to malign them, because they denied that baptism was repeated, inasmuch as infant baptism is no baptism at all. They called themselves simply Baptists, not re-Baptists. The offensive name was fastened on them in order to bring them under the penalty of the Justinian Code against the Donatists.

The Church, then, according to these so-called Anabaptists, must be a gathered society, to use the terminology later current among the Congregationalists, and cannot coincide with the community unless of course the community be restricted to adult believers, as was sometimes the case in Anabaptist colonies. An unweeded city like Zurich could never be regarded as the new Israel of God because Zwingli had not instituted a sufficient purge. The Church is to be kept pure by discipline and the expulsion of those who do not exemplify the pattern of Christ's conduct. The religious ban, however, was to be the only penalty. The arm of the state should never be invoked. Religious liberty was thus a tenet of the Anabaptists, and they were the first church to make it a cardinal point in their creed.

Furthermore church and state should be separate, inasmuch as the state is concerned with everyone in the community, whereas the Church consists only of the saints. The state was ordained because of sin, but the Church was created for the saved. These propositions entailed the dissolution of the whole structure of medieval society. Luther and Zwingli had never gone so far and recoiled the more because the Anabaptists went on to say that the true Christians must not only forswear an alliance with the state, but must have nothing whatever to do with it, since the world is the world and remains without hope of ever being Christianized. Luther agreed that society cannot be Christianized, but nevertheless believed that Christians must accept the office of magistrate in order to restrain outrageous villainy. The Anabaptists retorted that the state has indeed been ordained of God on account of sin and to restrain sin, but should be left to be administered by sinners.

Such a position of itself entailed a withdrawal from political life and the separation became all the more marked because the ethic of the Sermon on the Mount was taken literally and made incumbent upon all Christians. The Catholics took it literally but conserved it only through a vocational division whereby its rigoristic precepts applied solely to the monks. Luther rejected this division, insisting that Christian morality is demanded of all, but he regarded the Sermon on the Mount rather as a disposition than a code. The Anabaptists agreed with the Catholics in taking the counsels to the letter and with Luther as to the single standard. Hence all Christians became monks. There was this difference, however, that the Anabaptists did not reject marriage. They repudiated war and capital punishment. Under no circumstances would they wield the sword, nor would they go to law. They would take no oath, for Christ said "Swear not at all," and some held all things in common.

Their whole manner of life was summed up by a Swiss chronicler who was himself impressed although not persuaded: "Their walk and manner of life was altogether pious, holy, and irreproachable. They avoided costly clothing, despised costly food and drink, clothed themselves with coarse cloth, covered their heads with broad felt hats; their

THE CHURCH WITHDRAWN: ANABAPTISM 101

walk and conduct was altogether humble. . . . They carried no weapon, neither sword nor dagger, nothing more than a pointless bread knife, saying that these were wolf's clothing which should not be found on the sheep. They would never swear an oath, not even upon demand of the government. And if anyone transgressed, he was excluded by them."

Here, then, was a program not only of religious liberty and the separation of church and state, but also of pacifism and complete abstention from public life. The Anabaptists for the most part were not revolutionary — there were indeed a few marauders who because they left their children unbaptized were called Anabaptists, and there were a few among the early Anabaptists who would not go the whole way on the repudiation of the sword. The great majority, however, obeyed the government in matters not directly contrary to their tenets, disobeyed when conscience required, and suffered meekly whatever penalties were imposed.

Those who thus held themselves as sheep for the slaughter were dreaded and exterminated as if they had been wolves. They challenged the whole way of life of the community. Had they become too numerous, Protestants would have been unable to take up arms against Catholics and the Germans could not have resisted the Turks. And the Anabaptists did become numerous. They despaired of society at large, but they did not despair of winning converts to their way. Every member of the group was regarded as a missionary. Men and women left their homes to go on evangelistic tours. The established churches, whether Catholic or Protestant, were aghast at these ministers of both sexes insinuating themselves into town and farm. In some of the communities of Switzerland and the Rhine valley the Anabaptists began to outnumber Catholics and Protestants alike. Would not the growth of people with such views be even more of a menace to public security than the demolition of a city wall? In 1529 the imperial meeting at Speyer declared with the concurrence alike of Catholics and Lutherans that the death penalty should be inflicted upon the Anabaptists.

Menno Simons, one of their later leaders, reported the outcome.

Some they have executed by hanging, some they have tortured with inhuman tyranny, and afterwards choked with cords at the stake. Some they roasted and burned alive. Some they have killed with the sword and given them to the fowls of the air to devour. Some they have cast to the fishes. . . . Others wander about here and there, in want, homelessness, and affliction, in mountains and deserts, in holes and caves of the earth. They must flee with their wives and little children from one country to another, from one city to another. They are hated, abused, slandered and lied about by all men.

After recording the deaths of 2173 of the brethren, an Anabaptist chronicler proceeds:

No human being was able to take away out of their hearts what they had experienced. . . . The fire of God burned within them. They would die ten deaths rather than forsake the divine truth.

They had drunk of the water which is flowing from God's sanctuary, yea of the water of life. Their tent they had pitched not here upon earth, but in eternity. Their faith blossomed like a lily, their loyalty as a rose, their piety and candor as the flower of the garden of God. The angel of the Lord battled for them that they could not be deprived of the helmet of salvation. Therefore they have borne all torture and agony without fear. The things of this world they counted only as shadows. They were thus drawn unto God that they knew nothing, sought nothing, desired nothing, loved nothing but God alone. Therefore they had more patience in their suffering than their enemies in tormenting them.

ANABAPTIST MARTYRS

Their situation is poignantly described in an Anabaptist hymn:

> Sheep without shepherd running blind
> Are scattered into flight.
> Our house and home are left behind,
> Like birds we fly by night,
> And like the birds, naught overhead
> Save wind and rain and weather,
> In rocks and caves our bed.
>
> We creep for refuge under trees.
> They hunt us with the bloodhound.
> Like lambs they take us as they please
> And hold us roped and strong-bound.
> They show us off to everyone
> As if the peace we'd broken,
> As sheep for slaughter looked upon,
> As heretics bespoken.
>
> Some in heavy chains have lain
> And rotting there have stayed.
> Some upon the trees were slain,
> Choked and hacked and flayed.
> Drownings by stealth and drownings plain
> For matron and for maid.
> Fearlessly the truth they spoke
> And were not ashamed.
> Christ is the way and Christ the life
> Was the word proclaimed.
> Precious in Thy sight, O God,
> The dying of a saint.
>
> Our comfort this beneath the rod
> Whenever we are faint,
> In thee, O God, in Thee alone
> Are earthly peace and rest.
> Who hope on Thee, eternally
> Are sustained and blessed.

Few of those who had the temerity to attend an Anabaptist conference could expect to die in bed. Most of the more sober leaders were eliminated in a few years by fire, water, and sword. One has only to examine an Anabaptist hymn-book to see over against the names of the authors the notation: "Drowned 1525, burned 1526, beheaded 1527, hanged 1528," and so on. Sometimes whole congregations were taken; the leaders especially were struck down and the people left without a shepherd.

Then the less balanced spirits came to the fore. Those who had lived under the continual shadow of death in caves and desolate places of the earth began like Muentzer to dream dreams of the birds of the heaven coming to devour the carcasses of the oppressors, of the return of the Lord to vindicate the saints, of the New Jerusalem from which the 144,000 of the redeemed should go out to slaughter the ungodly. Whether the Lord would accomplish all this by Himself, or whether men should assist, was not alto-gether clear. Dates for the return of Christ were set and places selected as the New Jerusalem. Melchior Hoffman predicted that in the year 1533 he would be imprisoned for six months in Strasbourg and then the Lord would come. Only the first half of the prediction was fulfilled, and Hoff-man languished in prison, speedily forgotten even by his own party. But his ideas moved down the Rhine and in 1534 the town of Muenster in Westphalia was selected as the New Jerusalem. Here for the first and only time the Anabap-tists succeeded in taking over municipal government, and not without violence. Under all the strains pacifism suc-cumbed. The Anabaptists marched into the market place prepared to be as sheep for the slaughter, but armed with swords just as a reminder of what they might do if they chose. Whereupon a revelation from the Holy Ghost instructed them to choose that which they might. Catholics and Lutherans were expelled; the saints began their reign.

Leadership fell to those who sought to restore not only the New Testament but also the Old. They were like Zwingli in stressing the continuity between the new and the old Israel of God. But then they began to revive the eccentricities of the prophets and the immoralities of the patriarchs. Some Anabaptists in Holland ran around naked in imitation of the prophet Isaiah who walked naked as a sign. Another Anabaptist, also in imitation of Isaiah, went to the fireplace and lifted a hot coal to his lips. Instead of being able to say like the prophet, "Woe is me, I am undone, for I am a man of unclean lips," he was too burned to say anything for a fortnight. At Münster the aberration took the form of a reinstatement of polygamy after the example of Abraham, Isaac, and Jacob. Catholics and Lutherans combined to exterminate the New Jerusalem. The town was taken and all the new Davids and Enochs and Elijahs were put to the rack and the sword.

The whole ugly episode discredited Anabaptism. Despite the fact that for the first ten years under frightful provocation they had been without offense, yet when a handful of the fanatics ran amuck the entire party was besmirched with the excesses of the lunatic fringe, and well into the nineteenth century historians of the Reformation did little more than recount the aberrations of the saints rampant.

Despite constant vigilance Anabaptism was not extinguished. Nor did the excesses pervert the character of the movement as a whole. Menno Simons, the founder of the Mennonites, and Jacob Hutter, the founder of the Hutterites, repudiated all of the Muenster vagaries: polygamy, revolution, and date-setting for the return of the Lord. Anabaptism revived its original principles of a sect separated from the world, committed to following the pattern of the New Testament in simplicity, sobriety, poverty, meekness and long-suffering. Menno declared that true Christians must "crucify the flesh and its desires and lusts, prune the heart, mouth and the whole body with the knife of the divine word of all unclean thoughts, unbecoming words and actions." There must be no adornment with gold, silver, pearls, silk, velvet and costly finery. Swords must be beaten into plowshares and love extended even to enemies. Charity must be given to all, and though the faithful be despoiled of their goods they must turn not away.

For the most part in Europe these groups could find no abiding place. In Holland and Switzerland a few survived at the price of a measure of conformity. In Germany they were stamped out. This is one of the greatest tragedies of German history. If only Lutheranism could have been subject to the stimulus of the criticism and competition of the sects, it could never have become so complacent and allied to the established order. The Anglican Church owes an incalculable debt to the Nonconformists. So completely were the Anabaptists exterminated that few Lutherans are aware that the principles of British dissent originated on German soil.

The Anabaptists, however, do survive. They maintained themselves by following the frontier and keeping aloof from bourgeois civilization, industrialism, imperialism, and nationalism. They sought the fringes where social totalitarianism had not yet imposed conformity and the community of the saints could live unmolested. Poland and Moravia for a time offered an asylum. Tolerant noblemen were will-

ing to admit tillers of the soil without asking too many
questions about their religious convictions. In Moravia religious communist societies with an international complexion
were established in small groups of about a hundred. The
ideal was not the improvement of the standard of living
as in modern communism, but rather to live in accord with
Franciscan poverty but on a family basis. The resemblance
to monasticism is obvious save for celibacy and later the
Shakers were to introduce celibacy in a Protestant community, but the Mennonites and Hutterites have never done
so. How close they were, however, to monasticism appears
in the case of one group of Anabaptists in Moravia, who in
the period of the Counter Reformation were offered the
choice of exile or toleration of their entire mode of living
on the one condition that they accept the Mass. The Catholic Church regarded them as a quasi-monastic community.

Those who did not conform, and they were the majority,
had to suffer repeated exiles. Some went west, some went
east. Pennsylvania received a considerable migration. Other
bands traversed northern Germany to Poland, Hungary and
Transylvania and at length to Russia, until in the late nineteenth century new pressures in the east occasioned fresh
movements to the west, to Manitoba, Indiana, Nebraska,
and Paraguay. Eternal Abrahams, they have ever loins girt
ready to go they know not whither.

On the western frontiers the Anabaptists have preserved
their pattern more truly than in the Old World. During
the past four centuries they have succeeded amazingly in
maintaining a community life of their own, cut off from all
the corruptions of the world. The buttonless coats, the
broad hats, the flowing beards of the Amish set them apart
even on their occasional excursions into society. These

peculiarities serve like a uniform to distinguish the wearer and guard him against seduction. All the encroachments of modern society have been stoutly resisted — the railroad, the telephone, the automobile, the movie, the newspaper, especially the comic strips, and even the tractor. Naturally, too, the state school has been regarded as a peril to the community pattern. The old ways have been best preserved where the isolation is greatest and where the opposition is most acute. A segregated community thrives on persecution. It needs something like the ghetto for the preservation of its own morale. Contact with the outside and fraternization insidiously induce conformity. Then the children begin to dress and think like others and to go over to the world. The sect thus becomes the church and the old witness survives only in a warm piety and a nostalgic singing of martyr hymns.

The Reformed Church of Geneva: Calvinism

THE REFORMED CHURCH already evident in Zwinglianism presented a second and vastly more influential manifestation in Calvinism. These two forms were closely related geographically, the one originating in German and the other in French Switzerland, or to be exact in what is now French Switzerland, for at that time Geneva was an independent city. In idea the similarities were also great. Zwinglianism and Calvinism were alike parsimonious in the use of the external aids to religion. Images were by both rejected. Music was abandoned by Zwingli and restricted by Calvin. The concept of the Holy Commonwealth was common to both though Calvinism conceived it on a grander scale. In certain respects, however, Calvinism was more nearly related to the other two types of Protestantism. In regarding the Lord's Supper as a channel of spiritual communion the affinity was with the Lutherans, and the Calvinist psalm-singing was not remote from the Lutheran choral. At the same time the Anabaptist concept of the Church as a community of convinced believers and more notably the Anabaptist demand for a rigorous discipline left their imprints.

Yet Calvinism, though combining ingredients from Lutheranism, Zwinglianism, and Anabaptism, exhibited also differences. One was at the point of international dissemination and influence. The reason may have been in part that Calvin was a refugee at Geneva and lacked the sense of local attachment which bound Luther to Saxony and Zwingli to Zurich. But in part the explanation is that actually the door to expansion was closed to Lutheranism by Slavic orthodoxy to the east and the Counter Reformation to the south. The Anabaptists were internationally minded and had in their colonies frequently Germans, Czechs, Italians, and Poles, but the Anabaptists never captured the mind of any considerable portion of an entire country and cannot be said to have exerted an international influence.

The greatest difference lay in the activism of Calvinism. In a measure this was due to circumstances because the Calvinists were both under the necessity of action and not deprived of the possibility. They constituted in many lands minorities compelled either to be aggressive or to succumb, unlike the Lutherans who after the Peace of Augsburg in 1555 came to enjoy a recognized status and thereafter relaxed, and equally unlike the Anabaptists who were spewn to the fringes of Europe and could do no more than survive.

But the deepest reason for the activism of Calvinism lay in the realm of idea, and the idea originated with the man, John Calvin. He was a Frenchman and had his training in France in the days when the lines were not sharply drawn between humanist, Catholic, Reformed, and Lutheran. He was schooled as a humanist, and the orderliness of his thinking and the clarity of his diction may well be traceable to the influence of his classical studies. Liberal Catholics in France were deeply concerned for reform and to them

Calvin attached himself. Their treatment by the Crown depended on circumstance. Francis I was himself a humanist devoid of religious conviction, who alternately favored and suppressed incipient Lutheranism according to his need at the moment for an alliance with the Pope, the Turk, or the Schmalkaldic League. During one of the periods of pressure John Calvin saved himself by flight to Basel in Switzerland, and there, when only twenty-seven, brought out the book which was said to have made Protestantism intellectually respectable. This judgment is rather too disparaging toward Luther and Melanchthon, but none can deny to Calvin the palm for succinct, integrated, limpid exposition. His *Institutes of the Christian Religion* was for centuries to serve a large section of the Protestant worlá as the *Sentences* of Peter Lombard had served the Catholic. Even the *Summa* of Thomas Aquinas does not bear comparison, because it is too lengthy and intricate.

The *Institutes* of John Calvin set forth a view of God, man, and the Church which goes far to explain why Calvinism should have been the most active variety of Protestantism. The drive of Calvinism stems from optimism as to God despite pessimism as to man. Calvin's view of man was just as gloomy and, if anything, even more devastating than that of Luther and the Anabaptists. Zwingli, too, was much more generously disposed to the pious heathen. Calvin pictured man as vitiated in intellect and depraved in morals as a result of Adam's fall. The depravity, to be sure, in his view, was not complete at either point since the classical philosophers displayed a genius which excites our amazement, and among non-Christians there are assuredly varying levels of moral achievement. An upright pagan like Camillus is not to be compared with a reprobate pagan like

CALVINISTS VS. PAPISTS

Catiline. Nevertheless from the point of view of divine truth the philosophers, apart from God's revelation, are blinder than bats and moles, and apart from God's grace the virtues of the pagans are but splendid vices. Though the world without Christ need not be a pigsty, it will never be a paradise. From a similar analysis the Anabaptists deduced a necessary withdrawal of the Church from the world, and Luther allowed only a resigned participation. But Calvin came out with a resolute summons to action within the sphere of society.

The reason is to be found in his view of God. The great text for Luther was "Thy sins are forgiven," but for Calvin it was "If God is for us who can be against us?" Both Calvin and Luther had an overwhelming sense of the majesty of God, but whereas for Luther this served to point up the miracle of forgiveness, for Calvin it gave rather the assurance of the impregnability of God's purpose. Consequently the *Institutes* treat first of the sovereignty of God ahead of the section on justification by faith.

This God who is able to perform that which he has promised has a plan for mankind to be achieved within the historical process. Here is one of the most significant differences between Calvin and the previous reformers. He rejected their expectation of the speedy coming of the Lord and projected the final cataclysm into an indefinite future. Luther looked wistfully for the end of the age before his own demise and the Anabaptists often set dates. But Calvin renewed the role of St. Augustine who terminated the early Christian expectation of the speedy coming of the Lord and envisaged successive acts in the historical drama in which the Church came well-nigh to be equated with the kingdom of God. Even so Calvin substituted for the great and imminent day of the Lord the dream of the Holy Commonwealth in the terrestrial sphere.

Its erection depended upon human agents, God's chosen instruments, the elect. At first God's choice fell upon the Jewish people. In the commentary on Deuteronomy Calvin unrolled majestically the divine plan for Israel who by a mighty hand and an outstretched arm had been delivered from the hand of Pharaoh, led dry-shod through the Red Sea, conducted through the forty years in the wilderness, and brought to the borders of the land of promise where they should enter into an inheritance of wells which they had not dug and vineyards which they had not planted. This only was incumbent upon them that they should not forget the Lord their God but should bind his statutes as frontlets between their eyes, they and their children's children.

The people of Israel had failed in this great commission and in their stead God had selected the new Israel of God, the Christian Church. But this institution also had been recreant, and now only to a select few was the summons addressed, namely to the elect. Then came once more the question of the tests by which the elect could be known.

Luther did not pretend to know. Muentzer, Zwingli, and the Anabaptists had each a different test. The first said "by the spirit," the second "by faith," and the third "by the life." Calvin, like Luther, disclaimed absolute knowledge and did not aspire like the Anabaptists to compose the church of wheat and no tares. Nevertheless Calvin posited certain presumptive tests, in number three: profession of faith, an upright life, and participation in the sacraments. This means that he dropped entirely the test of Muentzer as too variable and subjective. It was to return later to plague New England Calvinism. He accepted Zwingli's test of faith and the Anabaptists' test of life. To these he added a third which relates him to Luther and even to the Catholics — namely, the test of participation in the sacraments.

All three tests were comparatively tangible. The profession of faith was less an inward experience than a public profession of the creed, an open declaration of the covenant or contract with God. The upright life was interpreted in the sense of austere deportment, abstention from dancing, card playing, gambling, obscenity, and drunkenness. The Calvinists derided the red nose of one of their persecutors in France and took a certain pride in their pale faces. Such discipline went far to justify the generalization that every Calvinist was a monk. The resemblance to Anabaptist standards is also quite obvious. Participation in the sacraments meant more than an initiation or a public testimonial to membership in a society as with the earlier Zwingli, because the sacraments for Calvin, as for Luther, were the channels of spiritual communion with God and the expressions of fellowship alike with Christ and with believers.

The man who by these tests is assured of election is utterly unshakable because he knows that his election "stands in the eternal and immutable good will of God towards us and that it cannot be altered by any of the storms of the world. . . . We should then cultivate a spirit of fortitude and courage which may serve to sustain us under the weight of all the calamities we may be called upon to endure, so that we may be able to testify to the truth that when reduced to the extremity of despair we have never ceased to trust in God."

Such confidence eliminated worry. The early Calvinist at any rate did not eat his heart out and consume his energies in concern as to his salvation. This point significantly sets off Calvinism alike from Catholicism and Lutheranism.

When Cardinal Sadoleto, the Catholic Bishop of Geneva, addressed to his lost parishioners a plea to abandon Calvin· ism on the ground that Catholicism offers a safer way of salvation, Calvin retorted that man should not be so pre- occupied with his salvation. The chief end of man is not to save himself or to be assured that he is saved, but to honor God. In any case man is already saved or damned and no worry will make any difference.

Calvin never openly discountenanced Luther's lifelong agonizing for faith, but the following passage might have been directed against it. Calvin declared, "It is not possible to serve God without a tranquil mind, for those who labor in inquietude, who dispute within themselves as to whether He is propitious or offended, whether He will accept or reject their prayers, those who in consequence waver be- tween hope and fear and serve God anxiously can never submit themselves to Him sincerely and wholeheartedly. Trembling and anxiety cause them to hate God and wish if it were possible that His very existence might be wiped out." For Calvin the doctrine of election was an unspeakable comfort because it eliminated all such worries and freed man from concern about himself in order that he might devote every energy to the unflagging service of the sovereign Lord. Calvinism therefore bred a race of heroes.

Their commission was to establish a theocracy in the sense of a Holy Commonwealth, a community in which every member should make the glory of God his sole con- cern. It was not a community ruled by the Church nor by the clergy nor even in accord with the Bible in any literalist sense, because God is greater than a book even though it contains His Word. The holy community should exhibit that parallelism of church and state which had been the ideal of the Middle Ages and of Luther, but had never been realized and never can be save in a highly select community where the laity and the clergy, the Town Council and the ministers, are all equally imbued with the same high purpose. Calvin came nearer to realizing it than anyone else in the sixteenth century.

To do so he needed a place, and he found it in Geneva. The city was not then a part of the Swiss Confederation but independent, because newly emancipated from the rule of the bishop and the Duke of Savoy, both of whom had been expelled. Their removal had been possible only through the help of the Swiss city of Bern which was Protestant. The first introduction of the Genevans to the Reform was when the Bernese stabled their horses in the Catholic churches and put images of the saints down the wells. Preaching followed when William Farel came in, a refugee from France, a fiery red-bearded Elijah bellowing at the priests of Baal. Civil war was only with difficulty averted and Geneva embraced the Reform. Farel felt himself very inadequate to hold the lid on the cauldron, for many Republicans who had taken arms to expel the duke and the bishop had no mind to submit to the yoke of the gospel. Then John Calvin passed through the town. For all his dream of a Holy Commonwealth the young theologian did not relish for himself the task of administering a turbulent city, but Farel threatened him with hell-fire and damnation if he did not dedicate himself to the will of the Lord. That plea was one which John Calvin could never resist. He stayed.

And then he endeavored to realize his program. Geneva should become the new Israel of God, like ancient Israel in covenant with the Lord and ready to stand for the purity of the worship of Jehovah against the seductions of Baal and the threats of the Moabites, the Amalekites, Philistines and Jebusites. The parallel was more than fanciful, since Geneva too was begirt by foes. The Duke of Savoy throughout the century did not abandon attempts to recover the city, and the Duke of Alva on his way to the Netherlands debated whether to stop on the way and sack Geneva. Like the company of Ezra and Nehemiah, Calvin's men labored in rebuilding the walls, sword in hand.

Within the city an effort was made to introduce a rigoristic regime which has often been the occasion of scoffing because it centered on what most people in a secularized culture have come to regard as trifles. There were penalties for having a fortune told by gypsies, for laughing during preaching, for making a noise in church, for passing tobacco during the service, for settling a bet on Sunday, for inability to recite prayers. Taverns were abolished and abbeys converted into hostels where no drinks were served on Sundays, during church hours on weekdays — for church was held on weekdays — nor after nine o'clock at night. With regard to all such regulations one must bear in mind that they were simply a continuation of the sumptuary legislation of the late Middle Ages which the Calvinists, with their newfound energy, proceeded to enforce.

Other regulations were designed to safeguard the purity of worship and were directed against the remnants of Catholic practices. A goldsmith was punished for making a chalice for the Mass, a barber for tonsuring a priest, another for saying the pope was a good man. The Genevan council even prohibited the Catholic practice of christening children with the names of Catholic saints or with such names as Cross, Jesus, Pentecost, Sunday, and Holy Sepulchre.

Such trivialities become always the butt of ridicule when they alone survive after the ideal is dead. But they were also the object of strong objection in Calvin's own day. The Republican party in Geneva was restive under the rod of "that Frenchman," as Calvin was called. He and Farel were banished for two years, but Calvin was recalled in 1541. He speedily recognized that his Holy Commonwealth could be realized only on a more sharply selective basis. The dissidents would have to go. The Catholic monastics had already been expelled even before Calvin arrived. We have a vivid account from a nun of how the syndic visited at the convent and the vicaress besought him to kill them all and get it over with. But he offered them martyrdom in the more excruciating form of matrimony. Only one nun accepted and the rest moved out of town. Otherwise Catholics were permitted to stay if they remained quiet. But even during Calvin's exile the Town Council undertook to eliminate any Catholics from the government. Jean Balard, a magistrate, was informed that on pain of banishment he must say "the Mass is bad." He replied, "that he is unable to judge but since it is the will of the Council that he say 'the Mass is bad' therefore he says 'the Mass is bad' and cries to God for mercy." This was not enough. He was permitted to stay only after he had affirmed without qualification, "the Mass is bad." Heretics were dealt with even more rigorously than Catholics. A denial of predestination meant banishment. A denial of immortality and the Trinity meant death. Gruet was beheaded and Servetus was burned. And those who opposed the regime on moral or political grounds were dealt with strenuously. A fracas in the streets was interpreted as a coup against the state. Some of the leaders were executed, some were banished. All open opponents of the Reform were thus excluded alike from the Church and from the city. Geneva was becoming a select community.

The process was further strengthened by the admission from the outside of those committed to the Holy Commonwealth. Refugees poured into the city. They came from Italy, from France, from Spain, and in waves from England. The Town Council was long hesitant to regard these strangers other than as wayfarers or at best as guests, but Calvin's persuasions at length prevailed, and the refugees became citizens. In the end as many as six thousand were taken into a city with an original population of thirteen thousand. Thus by the expulsion of dissenters and the inclusion of the conformists Geneva became a city of the saints.

The concepts of the Church embracing the entire community and of the Church as a sect comprising only the saved were thus combined. None but the convinced belonged to the Church but everyone in Geneva belonged to the Church because those who did not left the town. If one excommunicated did not make his peace with the Church within six months he was banished from the city. In this way Geneva came to resemble an Anabaptist colony except that the sword was not renounced and society was not abandoned.

From Geneva Calvinism spread into France, Holland, England, Scotland, and New England. The pattern of Geneva could not be reproduced in these lands, at least not at the outset. A single city might be turned into a select community. In the case of an entire land this was a very difficult matter. Eventually the ideal was most nearly achieved in Scotland and New England. In France, Holland, and old England Calvinism became rather a militant mi-

nority, a spiritual aristocracy over against the rest of the
population, though a democracy without gradations within
the body of the elect, a band of the chosen of the Lord,
calling no man sovereign save under God, not worrying
about salvation, sustained by the assurance of the unshakable
decree, committed not to the enjoyment of the delights of
life but only to the illustration of the honor of the sovereign
God, craving no recreation beyond the adventure of subduing kingdoms, beheading monarchs, taming wildernesses,
in order to erect the Holy Commonwealth, *le royaume de
Dieu.*

Tangible successes were not lacking in the Scotland of
the General Assembly, the England of Cromwell's protectorate and the New England of towns named Goshen, Dan,
Canaan, and Gilead. The holy commonwealths have come
and gone but they have left their residue in the still surviving faith that a nation can be Christian if the tone of its
public life and policy be set by a convinced, determined, and
upright minority of the elect.

7

The Free Spirits

THE REFORMATION OF THE SIXTEENTH CENTURY engendered another form distinct from the Lutheran, the Reformed, and the Anabaptist types. It was so amorphous, varied, and vague that it can better be described as a tendency than as a movement. The characteristic notes were mysticism and rationalism. Both are compatible with any of the previously established types of Christianity and both are subversive of it if exaggerated. Representatives of these attitudes were not very numerous in the sixteenth century and if quantity were the criterion of importance they might be omitted. Their significance lies in the pioneering of ideas which were subsequently to have an enormous vogue. The disciples of the free spirit, if they may be so designated, did very little by way of forming new churches, particularly because they could spiritualize the teachings and rites of any church, and preferred to remain where they felt at home unless expelled. If cast out, they were too indifferent to outward forms to set about the erection of new organizations. The one exception was Socinianism. As these tendencies were interconfessional, so were they also international. In all lands representatives were to be found, but the most outstanding were refugees from Spain and Italy, perhaps because those who react against an intransigent Catholicism not uncommonly find the conservative varieties of Protestantism an impossible halfway house and move out into the fields of free thought.

The mysticism and rationalism espoused by these free spirits are both deeply imbedded in the Christian tradition and both have proved alike fructifying and perverting. If mysticism means simply warm personal religion, then plainly no vital Christianity can be without it. But if mysticism be taken in the more technical sense as that type of religion which sees as its end the union of the human with the divine, then alike reinforcement and peril are implicit for Christianity. The notion that man may partake in the divine nature is found in the Second Epistle of Peter, and the Apostle Paul could quote with favor the heathen poet who said of God that in Him we live and move and have our being. Pursuing this idea the theologians of the early church appropriated the Greek concept of the attainment by mortal man of a blessed immortality through the discarding of humanity and the acquisition of divinity. Through union with God man becomes divine and immortal. So long as man remains man and God remains God these tendencies are entirely compatible with Christianity, but if the devotee is believed to be completely merged in the abyss of the Godhead, then the subject-object relationship, the polarity of the I and the Thou, so characteristic of the Hebrew-Christian tradition, is destroyed. The German mystic of the fourteenth century, John Tauler, went as far as he could in the mystical direction while safeguarding the Christian tradition with the analogy of a candle burning in the sunlight. The candle is still an individual flame, but its separateness is not apparent over against the light of the sun. Such mystical tendencies did not commend themselves to Luther, who could not conceive how weak and impure man could be merged in the purity of the All-Holy, and to Calvin the very notion of the deification of man was blasphemous. But many of the left wing found the mystic way congenial.

Another danger to Christianity in mysticism is the transmutation of history into myth. Christianity teaches that God actually became flesh in Christ Jesus and that the Bible has a unique value as the record of a unique revelation. But mysticism so emphasizes the constant accessibility of God as to render nugatory the historic manifestation of God in Christ. The life of the Master in consequence becomes rather an allegory of that which must take place in the inner life. The soul must be born again, die to sin and rise to newness of life. The Bible is valuable as testimony to an experience which can arise without the book and having arisen can dispense with it.

The other tendency with which mysticism was frequently combined was rationalism. This may seem strange because the warm and often ecstatic rapture of the mystic is foreign to the precision of cold logical analysis. The combination was possible through a division of spheres. Reason might operate to demonstrate the inadequacy of rival systems, including even those reared by reason itself, and then the diving board was ready for the mystic leap. Rationalism too, one must remember, is used in varying senses. There is the rationalism of a closely integrated system, such as that of Thomas Aquinas; but the term rationalism is more often applied to an attitude which is essentially irrational, at any rate anti-speculative. The rationalism of the Enlightenment defined reason in terms of common sense which lies within the range of the common man. This view of reason could be compatible with Christianity only if its scope were rigorously

limited and a majority of the Christian tenets declared to
lie in another domain. But if once the claim were made that
nothing in religion can be accepted which is not amenable
to common sense, then Christianity, which has always been
a laughingstock to the wise, is utterly undone. Sometimes
those who eschewed speculation engaged in controversy with
opponents on their own terms and entered into such precise
debate as to develop a rational irrationalism, thus creating
the illusion of a primarily speculative interest.

Mysticism and rationalism could combine partly by a
demarcation of sphere and partly through a coincidence of
interest. The rationalist aversion to theological niceties
could be undergirded by the mystic's indifference to credal
refinements. The *Imitation of Christ,* for example, declares
that the Trinity is better pleased by adoration than by speculation. Mysticism of course could and did develop a speculative interest of its own, directed not to the relations of the
three persons in the Godhead but to the eflux and reflux
of the aught and the naught. In this type of speculation
rationalism took no interest. The two combined mainly
because man is incurably religious and if the rationalist
undercuts the traditional faith he has nothing left to live
by unless he can establish a direct contact with the eternal.

The doctrines which mysticism and rationalism in the sixteenth century most commonly dissolved were those of the
Trinity, the vicarious atonement, and sometimes personal
immortality. The doctrine of the Trinity holds that God is
both a unity and a plurality. Within one essence there are
three persons, the Father, the Son, and the Holy Ghost.
They are sufficiently one that God is not three, and sufficiently distinct that God is not undifferentiated. But the
three can be held in unity only on the basis of that philo-

sophical doctrine of realism which affirms that deity is a universal, existing independently of particular manifestations. The doctrine of the Trinity cannot be philosophically defended on the basis of the Nominalist philosophy which regards reality as consisting only of unrelated particulars. In that case the three persons would have to be three distinct gods. This was the view held by the late Scholastics who were able to retain the doctrine of the Trinity not by logic, but only on the basis of churchly authority. When then that authority was weakened by the Reformation, the rationalists of the sixteenth century drew from the arsenal of these late Scholastics the weapons with which to demolish the doctrine. Mysticism reinforced their contentions because the abyss of the Godhead, so congenial to mystical thought, is not readily differentiated into three. And if it be held that emanations proceed from the abyss, as in Neoplatonic thought, then the problem is to arrest them at three.

The doctrine of the vicarious atonement, that God could not forgive the sin of man unless His justice were first satisfied by the substitutionary death of Christ, involved no logical difficulties. Here it was rather mysticism which was subversive because the great ocean of the Godhead which is ever ready to receive the human drop stands in no need of propitiation in order that this union may take place. The mystic lacked an intense sense of the purity of God and the impurity of man, and therefore felt no inner necessity for a moral satisfaction to be rendered to God.

The belief in immortality was imperiled by studies of the mind-body problem which pointed out that certainly no prior experience or analogy can demonstrate the possibility of the existence of the soul apart from the body. The doctrine therefore can be held only on faith. Here reason was to be a solvent. In the sixteenth century, however, the denial of immortality was never a common tenet.

Mysticism and rationalism, whether alone or in combination, pointed in the direction of universalism. Mysticism is actually found in all religions and can very readily conceive of Christianity as simply one among many valid approaches to God. And rationalism tends to reduce the teaching of Christianity to so simple a level that it is scarcely distinguishable from Stoicism and Confucianism. The religion of the Renaissance was very hospitable to a universal deism in which Christianity retained a nominal headship chiefly because already sublimated and transformed. Without any conscious attempt to abandon the faith, Renaissance mystics, notably the leaders of the Neoplatonic Academy at Florence, sought to discover the same set of truths beneath the symbols of many systems: in the lore of Zoroaster, the mysteries of the divine Hermes Trismegistus, in the alluring number speculations of the Jewish cabala. In such circles there were dreams of the reunion of all Christendom and even of a World Parliament of Religions. Tolerance became the watchword even at the expense of an emasculated Christianity.

Representatives of these tendencies were to be found in all lands. For this brief sketch single examples will have to suffice. For Germany, one may take Sebastian Franck. He was fond of talking of the nonpartisan God who does not and cannot allow Himself to be comprised within the categories of man because His being is so vast and so incomprehensible that it can be described only in terms of antinomies. Whatever is said of God, the opposite will also be true. This God makes himself known in partial measure to all men and not exclusively to a chosen few. Here the exclusiveness of the doctrine of election gives way to universalism. One is not surprised therefore to hear Franck say, "So far as human language can describe it, the Word of God is nothing other than an emanation, essence, outpouring, image, picture and appearance of God in all creatures, but especially in all surrendered hearts, illumining and teaching men from the beginning, Adam, Abel, Noah, Lot, Abraham, Job, Trismegistus, Mercury, Plotinus, Cornelius, and all the godly heathen." Universal theism enabled Franck to find fellows everywhere.

Wherefore my heart is alien to none. I have my brothers among the Turks, Papists, Jews, and all peoples, not that they are Turks, Jews, Papists and sectaries, or will remain so; in the evening they will be called into the vineyard and given the same wage as we. From the east and from the west children of Abraham will be raised up out of the stones and will sit down with God at His table.

Such a man could be at home in any church if he were permitted. Naturally Franck was not permitted. From a Catholic priest he became a Lutheran minister, and from a minister a layman, making soap to earn his bread. He had no mind to found a new church, for the true Church, said he, "is a spiritual invisible body of all the members of Christ, born of God in one mind, spirit and faith, not in one city or place outwardly assembled; a community in which we believe and do not see save with the eye of insight and of the inner man." The devotees of such a church are bound to be rejected of men and their only recourse is to make a cloister of their own hearts.

For France Guillaume Postel may serve by way of example. This amazing figure was consumed with an urge to unlock the mystic lore of the ancient East, and he began with the study of Hebrew. The King of France commissioned him to travel in the Orient under the aegis of the French mission at the Sublime Porte. In the course of his expeditions Postel discovered the apocryphal gospel of James, and acquired an acquaintance with Arabic, Syriac, and Aramaic. The Renaissance faith in the unity of all truth and the ultimate harmony of all faiths inspired him with a resolve to achieve the concord of all religions. The newly founded order of the Jesuits attracted him because they aspired to be simply "Jesusites," but they soon found his turgid spirit uncongenial and gave him a friendly dismissal. They had reason to be suspicious of a man whose aspirations after inclusiveness led him to assert that the revelation of God in Christ was inadequate because channeled through a male figure. Now the female manifestation was disclosed in the person of a certain Joanna who had nursed Postel through an illness in Venice. The Inquisition luckily declared him mad. Perhaps he was. But during an interlude of sanity he became for six months Regius Professor of Semitic Languages at the University of Vienna. Suspicion of heresy forced him to leave and he was delivered from the prisons of the Inquisition at Rome only by the death of the pope. He kept up close relations with the more radical of the Swiss Protestant reformers, the sectaries in Germany, and even with Anabaptists in Holland and Basel. Yet he was not done to death in Catholic France but lived to be seventy-one years of age and spent his latter days lecturing in a Parisian monastery on geography to an adulatory audience of literati. Here he died in the full odor of sanctity. During his life he had been wedded to many systems. Now whose shall he be in the classification?

For Germany and France these isolated examples must

suffice. For Spain and Italy the case is different. In these lands the free tendencies attracted greater numbers and attained in the end greater cohesion. A sketch of the religious situation in both countries is called for.

Spain was a land which had only attained national consolidation through the fall of Granada. Conquest was followed by conversion that there might be one monarch and one faith after the pattern of the Christian Roman Empire. Persuasion, bribery and force were employed to win the Moors and the Jews. Those who would not submit were expelled. The ships of Columbus starting for the New World passed the vessels carrying the Jews into the recesses of the Old. When the converts retained or relapsed into the practices of their former faith the Inquisition became an instrument of national policy and of national honor. Spain and orthodoxy were to be synonymous. The employment of the auto-da-fé to intimidate the recalcitrant must not, however, be allowed to obscure the fact that all Spain was pulsing with reform. In Spain originated the Catholic Reformation before ever the Protestant had begun. Ximenes antedated Luther.

Since force was used one might have expected that the *conversos* would have been cowed and sullen. Yet precisely among these groups we find an exuberant zeal manifesting itself in revivalism, prophesyings, and Messianism. Those who had embraced the faith from another background were not prepared to accept the established forms merely as a matter of tradition, and began instead to revive ecstatic elements present in the New Testament itself. In such circles the Protestant Reformation was not welcome because it was distinctly schismatic; it would rend the hard-won unity of Spain achieved by costly liberation from an alien yoke, and would sever her from the body of that Europe for which so long she had yearned. But if Lutheranism was unacceptable, Erasmianism was avidly received.

The reason was partly political. Erasmus was a Hollander and the Low Countries at that time were under the rule of the Spanish Hapsburgs. Charles V spoke by preference Flemish. Many in his court were from the Netherlands. In this circle Erasmus was an idol. He himself embodied in a measure the two tendencies which were to go into the movement of the free spirits. He had been nurtured by the Brethren of the Common Life and shared in their disparagement of scholastic speculation and in their exaltation of the spirit against the outward and ceremonial manifestations of religion. He was also something of a rationalist in his desire to reduce Christianity to the simple and readily intelligible and easily known. He decried discussion of such thorny problems as the Trinity which might better be deferred until the judgment day. He was an expert in the application of critical principles to the source books of Christianity. His universalism made him hospitable to the pious heathen. Along with Erasmus came also Dutch and German writings more definitely mystical. In this period Tauler was introduced into Spain. In the 1520's, then, when Luther was sweeping Germany, Erasmus was molding the mind of the Hispanic Peninsula and of the Spanish missions in the New World. One of the most popular books in Spain was the *Enchiridion* in which Erasmus derided those who made more of a bone of the Apostle Paul enshrined in a silver casing than of the spirit of the Apostle shining through all his writings. In remote Mexico the works of Erasmus were turned into Aztec for the religious instruction of the natives.

But only until 1530 was this vogue to last. Europe was being sharply severed into hostile camps. Erasmus himself fled from Catholic Louvain to save himself from being turned into an inquisitor; he sought refuge in Basel until Protestant excesses drove him again to Catholic Freiburg, where Catholic intolerance alienated him to the point of return to Basel. He averred insistently his desire to escape Scylla and Charybdis, but the gap between them grew too narrow for the slenderest bark. The day had come for an "either . . . or" and Spain was clear where she would stand.

The Inquisition began to spread its net for all those of liberal leanings. Some even of militant orthodoxy found themselves enmeshed, for example Archbishop Carranza of Toledo. Though under Philip II he was employed to hound heretics and himself aided in the formulation of the decrees of the Council of Trent, yet in the 1560's his own orthodoxy was impugned and only after seventeen years of incarceration was he vindicated. Professor Vergara at the University of Alcalá was so conscious of his rectitude as to be contemptuous of the Inquisition. From prison he communicated with the outside by letters written on wrapping paper with fruit juice. His ruse was discovered and he was detained during four years for contempt if not for heresy. The works of Erasmus in the 1530's were placed upon the Index and his woodcut portrait after Holbein was defaced by the scribe of the Inquisition. The Erasmians succumbed and the Jesuits triumphed.

Yet out of Spain came a few exiles who exercised a disproportionate influence beyond their native land. The first was Michael Servetus. He came from a rigorously orthodox family. His own brother, a beneficed priest, was willing in later years to cross the Pyrenees in order to lure him into the toils of the Inquisition. As a student in France, Servetus became exercised over the problem of the Trinity. His concern was practical, because in his judgment this doctrine constituted the primary obstacle to the conversion of the Moors and the Jews. What then was his surprise and relief when amid student groups searching the Scriptures under Protestant influence, he discovered in the Bible not one word about the three persons in one essence! He was curious then to discover how this doctrine had arisen and set himself to examine the writings of the late Scholastics, the Nominalists, who, committed to the view that reality consists only of unrelated particulars, were forced to regard the three persons of the Godhead as three gods from the philosophical point of view, though from the theological point of view as one God because the Church had so decreed. Servetus had been weakened, however, in his faith in churchly authority through infiltrating Protestant criticism, and could not therefore accept on authority in theology that which for philosophy appeared false. With avidity he seized upon the acids of decadent scholasticism to corrode the doctrine which he could not find enunciated in Scripture and which he conceived to be the chief obstacle to the religious unification of Spain.

His own view was a curious blend, remote from the modern desire to make of Jesus a man like other men. His denial was simply of the eternity of the Son of God. The Son, he said, was not eternal because the Son was a combination at a given point in time of the eternal Word and of the man Christ Jesus. This Christ after the union became the Light of the World, the immanent form of light investing all creatures with visibility. Not the reduction of Christ to the level of humanity but the exaltation of humanity to the

THE TRINITY AS THREE DISTINCT MEN

level of Christ was the core of the religion of Servetus. Like the ancient Greek theologians, he held that man is able to put off mortality and be clothed in immortality only if he first put off humanity and acquire divinity through union with the divine man, the Son of the eternal God. This was the view which Calvin found even more execrable than the denial of the Trinity because for Calvin God was so utterly transcendent that any such blending of the human and the divine was for him an unthinkable sacrilege. With such speculations Servetus combined the rejection of infant baptism and also the radical dream of the restitution of primitive Christianity. These heresies Servetus would have expiated at the stake in Catholic France had he not escaped and paid the same penalty in Protestant Geneva. After his execution Calvin received the news that the views of Servetus were spreading in Italy. Thither Servetus would have gone had he lived.

Another Spanish reformer who did go to Italy was Juan Valdez, a brother of the imperial secretary, an Erasmian with a still deeper mysticism drawn directly from men like Tauler. Valdez in his lodge on the island of Ischia conducted retreats attended by the Italian aristocracy, high dignitaries of the Church, women of refinement and cultivated tastes. He was to them a spiritual father discoursing on the vanity of all outward show, including even monastic austerities and macerations of the flesh, since nothing matters save the glow of the spirit and nothing keeps us from God save our own stubborn self-will. There is no need that God be placated by the sacrifice of Christ. The purpose of that sacrifice was not to pay a debt to the justice of God but to satisfy the crude notions of men who were impeded from coming to God because they supposed they could not be forgiven unless the debt were paid. Therefore to appease human concern about divine justice God sent his Son to make expiation. Obviously by such a view the doctrine of the vicarious atonement was undercut.

The Italy into which the views of Servetus and Valdez entered was very ambiguous in its attitude toward the Church of Rome. In one sense Rome was the glory of Italy, a city-state made resplendent by the Renaissance and drawing to itself great wealth from the north. To abolish the papacy would extinguish the greatest light in Italy. At the same time papal pretensions were resented. The city-states often quarreled and sometimes fought with the popes. The sectarianism in the late Middle Ages had flourished especially in the north of Italy; and its spirit was by no means extinguished. Witness the rise of the Capuchins in the sixteenth century! They were a Catholic monastic order who managed to remain within the fold, but they had drunk heavily from the literature of the spiritual Franciscans from whom had gone forth the schismatic Fraticelli. The early Capuchins had all the spirit of those who had put the rule of St. Francis above a decree of any pope.

Italy was at the same time the mother of the Renaissance. Here flourished the critical temper of Lorenzo Valla, the exposer of spurious documents. Here likewise were cultivated the mystical tendencies of the Florentine Academy. Italy thus combined sectarian, rationalist, and mystical currents before the advent of the Reform. In such soil Lutheranism took hold especially in the north, and the number of those converted back to the Catholic faith at the end of the century by the Capuchins demonstrates that the movement must have been more widespread than contemporary evidence enables us to fix with precision.

For a time there were high churchmen imbued with ideals strangely compounded of Luther and Erasmus. There were some even who were prepared not only to acknowledge and reform the monstrous moral abuses but who would concede in the doctrinal area the Lutheran tenet of justification by faith. But in Italy as in Spain the lines began to be drawn more sharply. The last conference with the Protestants was held in 1541 and although Cardinal Contarini conceded justification by faith, his work was repudiated and he came home to die. The following year, 1542, saw the organization of the Roman Inquisition, and in 1545 began the sessions of the Council of Trent. In Italy as in Spain liberals, even among the cardinals, were cast into the dungeons of the Inquisition.

Then the Italian liberals divided into three groups. There were those who retired into cloisters or who made cloisters of their own hearts, spiritualizing after their own manner the rites and the teaching of the Church. But only those who died early were able to do this. After the inquisitors became too adroit to tolerate any subterfuges, the choice then lay only between death or exile.

Among the exiles we find the only permanent residue of the Italian form of the Reformation. In it were prominent the mystical and rational ideas already characteristic of the Italian Renaissance and more definitely formulated by the Spaniards, Servetus and Valdez. But the Italians went further than the Spaniards in establishing a community, perhaps because in Italy the sectarian influence had been so potent. Northern Italy had conventicles marked alike by Antitrinitarian and Anabaptist ideas. Thus the Free Spirits from the Latin lands gravitated to the leftist groups of the northern climes.

Of course neither on Catholic nor on Protestant soil in that age could any refuge be found for such ideas. The only available haven, before the opening of the New World to migration, was along the eastern border of Europe, where surviving feudalism made possible that diversity which is crushed by the modern national states. A Polish noble might, if he wished, offer an asylum to the persecuted without himself suffering intimidation from the crown.

Poland then became the great center for those who variously combined Antitrinitarian and Anabaptist views. The movement in this country came to be known as Socinian from Faustus Socinus, or better Sozzini. The advent of the Italians was facilitated by the favor of the Queen of Poland, Bona Sforza, herself obviously an Italian. Under her patronage cultural connections with Italy were pursued and by the same route heresy entered. The degree of organization achieved by these religious communities was not rigid. The anomaly is that Faustus Socinus was the acknowledged spokesman of a church from which he was excluded. Theologically he is commonly represented as a rationalist and rightly so to a degree in that he appropriated from Servetus the old scholastic attacks on the doctrine of the Trinity, and with Valdez he repudiated the idea of the vicarious atonement. A strain of mysticism is commonly overlooked, but it is significant that the great Socinian statement of faith, the Racovian Catechism, posits as the chief end of man the attainment of incorruptibility and immortality. Here is a survival of the concept, so congenial to Eastern orthodoxy and often occurring in Western mysticism, which seeks to make Christ closer to men in order that through him they may be brought closer to God and thereby acquire the divine characteristic of deathlessness. On the score of social ethics, Socinianism shared with the Anabaptists repudiation of the oath and an aversion to war.

The Socinian movement found a footing not only in Poland but also in Hungary, Moravia, and Transylvania, lands intermittently subject to the Hapsburgs and the Turks. The Protestant outcasts preferred the infidels to the Catholics, because the unbelievers were more tolerant. In these border lands Protestantism thus became in a sense anti-European, ready at any rate to divide Europe into two camps not only in the field of religion but even also in the field of politics.

The Free Spirits, though leaving after them little by way of organized movements, stamped nevertheless their imprint upon other Protestant bodies at the point of critical inquiry, mystical piety, and religious liberty. The Age of the Enlightenment raised few monuments to forgotten precursors but stood none the less in their debt.

8

The Fight for Recognition
of the Lutheran Faith

THE EMERGENCE OF ONE RIVAL, let alone four, to the Catholic Church disrupted the structure not only of the religious but also of the social and political life of the Middle Ages. The process was accelerated by the coincident disintegration of the Holy Roman Empire through the forces of nationalism. This served also to undercut the universal jurisdiction of the Catholic Church. Long before the Reformation in most Catholic lands nationalism had subordinated the Church and implemented it to the ends of national unity. Gallicanism in France was the system whereby appointments to ecclesiastical benefices, and allocation of ecclesiastical wealth, were directed more from Paris than from Rome. Similarly in Spain the sovereigns manipulated church affairs sometimes in defiance of papal directives, and the Inquisition itself was pressed into the service of the state as an instrument of national honor. The direction was toward national churches as to externals while these churches at the same time remained spiritually subject to Rome.

But the new national states, though desirous of curbing the papacy, were of no mind to tolerate more than one religion in their domains. *Une foi, un roi, une loi* — one faith, one king, and one law — was still the model for any sound body politic, and those lands like Sweden and England which broke with Rome had no intent to allow more than one variety of Protestantism, let alone to permit Catholic minorities. One form only of the new religion was established and all else proscribed. The national states were to be smaller replicas of the medieval system. A very serious problem was then created if some of the populace were Catholic and some Lutheran, and a still more serious complication if in addition there were Zwinglians, Calvinists, Anabaptists or Socinians. The city of Augsburg, for example, toward the middle of the century had four parties: Catholic, Lutheran, Zwinglian, and Schwenkfelder, from Kaspar Schwenkfeld, one of the spiritual reformers.

The political strains arising from the religious tension of rival confessions could be eased in one of several ways. Ultimately the most satisfactory was complete religious liberty. This method was approximated in Poland in 1573 when Lutherans, Calvinists, and Hussites, having failed to achieve agreement, agreed nevertheless to differ. The term *Pax Dissidentium* was applied to their accord, the peace of those who agree to differ. But the balance in Poland was soon upset by the Counter Reformation. Not until the next century did Holland and England approximate this scheme, though still with restrictions as to the number of the varieties to be included in the settlement.

In the sixteenth century people did not commonly agree to differ. Then the choice lay between two other methods. The first was that of territorial division according to the principle of *cuius regio eius religio* — "whose region his religion" — meaning that the religion of a particular territory should be determined by the civil ruler. No competing cult was accorded the right of public worship, but dissenters were free to emigrate to a region of their own faith. Germany was eventually divided in accord with this principle, and the American colonies perforce adopted the same plan because the different confessions carved out for themselves separate principalities; and even the Federal Constitution provided only that there should be no national establishment of religion, but left the colonies free to continue the union of church and state, which lasted in certain localities as late as the eighteen-thirties.

The third solution was that of comprehension. It has certain of the characteristics of the other two. Only one religion is recognized in a given territory but in order to reduce emigration the attempt is made to satisfy as many as possible by making only minimal demands. The doctrinal and liturgical requirements are whittled down to such slenderness that only the ultra-scrupulous will decline conformity and the way of assent is further facilitated because the necessary tenets are so clothed in a garment of ambiguity that each can place upon them his own construction in a spirit of latitude. This was the solution at which Charles V in the Augsburg Interim made a faltering and unsuccessful attempt. Subsequently Queen Elizabeth in England was at once more drastic and more successful, despite the non-conformity of Catholic Recusants and Protestant Dissenters.

The struggles, the wars, the abortive attempts and the permanent residues in the meeting of the problem call for a review country by country and confession by confession. Broadly speaking the struggle in Germany and Scandinavia was for the recognition of Lutheranism; in France, the Netherlands, and Scotland primarily of Calvinism; in England of a middle way with a Calvinist tinge; in Italy and

Spain there was never a serious possibility of any competitor to Catholicism. In the eastern lands, Poland, Hungary, Moravia, and Transylvania, a number of sects contended on well-nigh equal footing.

This chapter will review the situation in Switzerland by way of prelude and then will deal with the struggle of Lutheranism in Germany and the lands to the north. The next chapter will take up the fight of the Calvinist groups.

In Switzerland, to recapitulate, the adoption of the Reform first by Zurich and then by other of the northern cantons threatened to split the confederacy. The Catholics turned for help to the Hapsburgs and the Protestants to the German Lutherans. The upshot was civil war, twice over, in 1529 and in 1531. On the second occasion Zwingli lost his life. The resulting peace was more generous to the Protestants than might have been expected. The territorial principle was adopted within Switzerland. Those areas in which the Reform was already entrenched were not to be disturbed. The Catholic minorities must be tolerated. In Catholic lands, however, evangelical missionary activities should cease and Protestant minorities were not to be allowed. The invidious consequences of this peace became apparent in the early fifteen-fifties when an entire community at Locarno in Catholic Switzerland was converted to Protestantism. The Diet of the Swiss Confederation met as a unit with representatives of the Protestant and Catholic cantons side by side. The problem before them was the way in which to enforce the peace of Kappel which forbade any further infiltration of Protestantism into Catholic lands. The law would authorize the Catholics to clear their territory by a blood purge. To obviate this some of the Protestant cantons proposed banishment for the Locarno community. But

CAROLO RO. REGI

VICTORIA

EMPEROR CHARLES V

Zurich would not concur in the infliction of any penalty whatever for the profession of her own faith. Her evangelical colleagues in the diet pointed out that such disclaiming of responsibility meant consigning the lambs to the wolves. The upshot was that the entire community migrated and settled in Zurich. That was how the Pestalozzi family came to be German Swiss. In this way Switzerland anticipated on a small scale the territorial solution with the *ius emigrandi,* the right of emigration. Thereby the political unity of the Confederation was saved.

In Germany the problem at first was what to do with Martin Luther, whether or no to enforce the Edict of Worms, but when his following increased the problem came to be as to competing confessions. The emperor was never of two minds on the subject. Increasingly he thought of himself not so much as the King of Spain or the head of the House of Hapsburg as in the role of a universal monarch commissioned by heaven to reform, restore, and protect the Holy Catholic Church. But Charles's hands were never free. To his dismay he discovered obstruction in Rome itself. The popes did not abet his aspirations to universal monarchy, nor did they welcome his plan for reform through a general council summoned and conducted under imperial auspices. So great was the conflict between the head of the empire and the head of the church that in 1527 Rome was sacked and the pope actually was captured by the imperial troops. Charles found himself then for a time in a position to dictate to the pope — but only for a time because a pope under duress is not a pope, and Charles discovered that if he were to retain his advantage he must renounce it and rely upon subtler methods to manipulate St. Peter.

Another obstacle lay in France, abetted on occasion by England, for these national states had no mind to see the Hapsburgs entrenched in Spain, Naples, and the Netherlands and reinforced by the imperial dignity exercising a European hegemony. French policy strove continually to gain northern Italy, to control the left bank of the Rhine, and to weaken the Hapsburgs in the Low Countries. Only in the wake of ignominious defeat would the French recognize the emperor as the lord of Europe, and such abject surrender never lasted long.

The Turks were the third great menace. Not only did they harass the Mediterranean but during much of this period they were encamped on the outskirts of Vienna and held

Hungary as a satellite state. Charles was fired with crusading zeal to unite all Europe for the expulsion of the infidels. But the pope, who often enough issued such appeals in his own name, was so far from endorsing an imperial crusade that on occasion he was actually willing to join in an alliance with the French and Turks.

Charles could not count with absolute assurance even on those domains in which he was the hereditary lord. Disorders from time to time rocked Spain. Anabaptism, the most virulent form of Protestantism, infested the Netherlands and infiltrated even into Austria. In Germany, over which Charles ruled as emperor, there were conflicting currents. On the one hand the Germans had deep respect for the empire and the opposition of the Lutherans was continually impeded by scruples of conscience. On the other hand, there was jealousy of the Hapsburgs and even the most Catholic princes would hesitate to adopt severe measures against the heretics if any advantage would thereby accrue to the House of Hapsburg. As a result of these many complications, Charles for twenty-five years was not in a position to throw full weight into the struggle for the extermination of heresy in Germany, and he was too prudent a ruler to have recourse to extreme measures unless he were in a position to back them up. The outcome was oscillation between attempts at solution by coercion and by conciliation. During the long period of vacillation Lutheranism gained such a footing that in the end conciliation was the only live alternative.

In the 1520's the problem centered at least formally upon the disposition to be made of Luther and the Diet of Nürnberg in 1524, meeting in the absence of the emperor, contented itself with the ambiguous formula that "the Edict of Worms should be enforced in so far as might be possible," which in practice left the evangelical territories at liberty to disregard it. The next diet met at Speyer in 1526. In the meantime the problem had already begun to shift from the man to the party because a political Protestantism began to emerge under the leadership of Philip of Hesse, actuated by the resolve to have recourse if need be to military measures in case interference should be attempted. The diet decreed that each ruler should demean himself "as he would have to answer to God and the Emperor," which to all practical intent asserted the territorial principle. So matters were left for three years during which time a number of the south German cities became Lutheran, including Strasbourg, Augsburg, Ulm, Nürnberg, and Constance. When the next diet met in 1529, also at Speyer, the evangelicals had been weakened because Philip of Hesse had been betrayed by forged misrepresentation of Catholic plans into making overtures to the traditional enemies, France and Bohemia. Many loyal Germans were thereby alienated, and the diet in consequence endorsed territorialism with a balance in favor of the Catholics. The Edict of Worms should be enforced in their lands, but provisionally, until the meeting of the next General Council; Lutheranism should be tolerated in those regions where it could not be suppressed without tumult. In Lutheran lands the principle of religious liberty must apply to Catholic minorities, but a similar standing would not be conceded to Lutheran minorities in Catholic lands. Against the invidiousness of this arrangement the evangelicals protested: hence the origin of the name Protestant. The word is unfortunate as a name because it implies that Protestantism was mainly an objection. The dissenters in their own statement affirmed that "they must protest

and testify publicly before God that they could do nothing
contrary to His word." The emphasis was less on protest
than on a witness.

The respite, such as it was, lasted but for a year during
which time Philip of Hesse sought to unite the Lutherans
and the Swiss in the hope of extending a military alliance.
In this he failed, and on the other side the emperor, having
humbled the French and the pope, found himself free to
come to Germany to deal with the religious issue. He was
resolved to try first the gloved hand, and if unsuccessful
to use the mailed fist. The question was to be settled by a
diet meeting at Augsburg in 1530. This was not a church
council nor even a gathering primarily of theologians. Luther
could not be present because he was still under the ban
of the Empire. The leadership on the theological side was
taken by Melanchthon who drafted the Augsburg Confession. It was an attempt to stress all the common elements
between Lutheranism and Catholicism in the hope that
an understanding could be achieved. Papal authority even
was not expressly rejected. But on the doctrinal side justification by faith alone was asserted and transubstantiation
denied.

How many of the Protestant varieties would endorse the
Augsburg Confession was a question to be determined.
For a time it looked as if it would not be the common
statement even of all Lutherans, but only of the Saxons.
In the end, however, all of the Lutherans gave their adherence, including even Philip of Hesse. The Swiss, however, submitted a separate statement; so also did the south
German cities. The Anabaptists, who at the Diet of Speyer
in 1529 had been subjected to the death penalty with the
concurrence of the Lutherans, were naturally not given an

AUGSBURG IN THE SIXTEENTH CENTURY

opportunity to be heard at all. Protestantism was not able
to present a united front, but at least the Lutherans were one.

The conciliatory spirit in which they stressed all that
they held in common with Rome did not mollify the papacy.
The denial of transubstantiation was enough in itself to
make the Augsburg Confession unacceptable. The theologians had done their utmost to avert conflict. The time
had now come for the princes to make their confession.
This they did with such steadfastness as to show that
Protestantism was no affair merely of ministers and profes-
sors nor even of pious conventicles. The lay rulers of the
territorial states also were ready "to let goods and kindred
go, this mortal life also." When George of Brandenburg
was threatened by the emperor should he refuse to par-
ticipate in the Corpus Christi procession, the margrave an-

swered, "Before I let any one take from me the word of
God and ask me to deny my God, I will kneel and let him
strike off my head." Charles was not prepared for such
extreme measures. He agreed to tolerate the Augsburg
Confession for a year. If at that time the Lutherans did
not submit they should feel the edge of the sword. The
significance of the whole occasion was the unification of
Lutheranism, the stand of the lay leaders, and the concession of a temporary recognition to a rival of the Catholic
Church. Henceforth in practice Germany was to be a land
of two confessions.

But another fifteen years had to go by before this solution
received definitive recognition. When the year expired
Charles was not in a position to make good his threat of
force, nor indeed for more than ten years was he able to

deal with the question again. And then his hands were
still so tied that conciliation appeared wiser than constraint.
Long had he been harping on the need for a church council,
and consistently the popes had obstructed. The pope at
last began to realize the folly of a course which by default
transferred the discussion of ecclesiastical matters to the
German diets, which were lay tribunals. So had it been
since the close of the fifth Lateran Council in 1517. After
well-nigh a quarter of a century the pope consented to
the summoning of an ecclesiastical council at Regensburg
in 1541. Protestants and Catholics were in attendance and
the purpose was to see whether accord could be achieved
There was some real hope because the leader of the Catholic
side was Cardinal Contarini, one of the Italian liberals of
the Erasmian brand, and the leader on the Protestant side
was Martin Bucer of Strasbourg, noted for his mediatory
role between the Swiss and the Lutherans. The cardinal
doctrine of Luther, justification by faith, proved after all
not to be an insuperable obstacle because Contarini was
ready to accept it, though whether he meant by it precisely
what the Lutherans did is another matter. But the Protestant
rejection of transubstantiation was more serious and Bucer,
unlike Melanchthon at Augsburg, was very insistent on the
rejection of papal authority. Union failed, and even the
concessions which Contarini had made were repudiated
after his return to Italy. The broken mediator died shortly
thereafter, the last great exponent of a transient hope.

The day of the liberal at Rome was done. The Roman Inquisition was introduced in 1542. The implacable Caraffa,
the Calvin of the Counter Reformation, received the tiara
as Paul IV in 1555, committed alike to the extermination of
immorality and heresy. He was sustained by new monastic

orders: the Capuchins, who after the defection of their general Ochino to the Reform became strictly regimented· the Theatines, an order of priests dedicated to pastoral care and ascetic demeanor; and above all others, the Jesuits, the epitome of Spanish reform purged of all Erasmian elements. The pope at last did summon a council at Trent which was to continue in session for twenty years, and throughout that time increasingly under papal control.

All hopes for a solution of the religious difficulty by agreement were definitely blasted. Of the three plans variously attempted in the sixteenth century, the *Pax Dissidentium* least of all commended itself to Charles because toleration was remote from his presuppositions, and territorialism almost equally violated his universal aspirations. Comprehension remained in the form of an imposed compromise. Before announcing the nature of the settlement Charles desired to place himself in a position to enforce it, and began therefore to gird himself for a military onslaught. His venture was bold, not to say heroic, at a time when France, Scotland, Denmark, Sweden, Juelich-Cleve, and the Turks were in league against him. All Germany save Bavaria either had been or appeared to be on the point of embracing the Reform. The Protestants under the lead of Philip of Hesse had discovered at last a formula of concord in 1536 between the Lutherans and the Swiss, and had forged a formidable military weapon in the Schmalkaldic League, which operated on home soil, whereas Charles had to import troops from Spain. Nevertheless the emperor succeeded by diplomacy, war, and sheer luck, in dissipating his enemies.

He was swift to exploit the ambitions and the foibles of his foes. Maurice of ducal Saxony was bribed to be neutral by a transfer of the electoral dignity from the other branch of the Saxon line to his own. Philip of Hesse was paralyzed by the scandal of his bigamous marriage which made him a suppliant for imperial grace because of the breach of the imperial law. The leadership of the resistance devolved upon electoral Saxony where scruples over the impropriety of armed rebellion impeded a war without reserve.

Either through conviction or inefficiency the Schmalkaldic League let slip opportunities to crush the emperor. A war of attrition ensued in which Charles proved to have the longer wind. Although his troops were wasted by disease he was better able to supply pay than the Schmalkaldic League. By November 1545 the army of the League dissolved. One by one the south German cities capitulated. Actual battle decided the issue in the north. John Frederick, the elector of Saxony, was captured and condemned to death. His sentence was then commuted to life imprisonment. Philip of Hesse surrendered, expecting to be treated as a prince; instead he was made a prisoner.

Then Charles announced his policy of comprehension embodied in the *Interim*, so called because it should be valid during the interim until a definitive solution could be achieved by a general council. The Protestants were granted but two concessions and both in the practical rather than in the doctrinal sphere. The cup in the Mass might be given to the laity and priests might marry.

Almost to a man the Protestants refused to have anything to do with such a scheme of comprehension. Luther was dead but his teaching had now taken such deep root that four hundred evangelical ministers in south Germany forfeited their livings rather than comply. A number like Bucer went into exile, and then congregations without their ministers carried on. The Reformation plainly was not a system imposed on people by governmental agencies from above but rather the expression of a faith not to be uprooted by the hand of man. Even Maurice of Saxony was so outraged by the treatment accorded the captive princes that he shook off his neutrality and struck with such swiftness that the emperor succeeded barely in saving his person while losing his dream.

A universal solution of the religious problem had failed. Charles resigned from the Empire and retired to a monastery in Spain, there to rehearse the funeral for which he had but two years to wait. The unraveling of the German tangle was left to his brother Ferdinand. Territorialism was the only possible solution remaining, and this was the principle of the Peace of Augsburg in 1555. For the first time in the Christian West two confessions, the Roman Catholic and the Lutheran of the Augsburg Confession, were given equal legal recognition. The Zwinglians, Calvinists, and Anabaptists were excluded. The secularization of ecclesiastical properties up to 1552 was regularized. For the future the religion of a territory should be determined by the ruler and minorities should be free to emigrate. The answers to two important questions remained ambiguous. The Catholics insisted that if an ecclesiastical domain should subsequently turn Protestant, the goods should remain with the Catholic Church. The Protestants did not concur. They in turn expected that Lutherans should enjoy toleration in Catholic lands, but this was not stipulated. Such ambiguities, plus the restriction of toleration to Lutherans only among the Protestants, contributed materially to the outbreak of the Thirty Years' War. But something at any rate had been gained. The principle of ecclesiastical solidarity was broken. Those who deplore any breach in unity as scandal and sin will bemoan the outcome. Those who prize liberty above universality will see here one step in the direction of freedom in religion.

Lutheranism in Germany had achieved a position of equality alongside of Catholicism. In the Scandinavian countries Lutheranism was to displace Catholicism as the established church. The primary motive was political, a phase of the trend toward the erection of national churches whether under nominal Roman suzerainty or with severance. Doctrine played an inconsiderable role in comparison with the efforts of the crown to appropriate ecclesiastical wealth and to control ecclesiastical appointments. The upshot was the establishment in Sweden of the first Protestant national church in 1527, a full six years before the founding of the Anglican Church. All of this is not to deny genuine religious interests. The Scandinavian lands, like the rest of Europe, had in the early years of the sixteenth century numerous reformers of an undifferentiated complexion, capable of alignment either with Catholic or Protestant reform. The proximity of Germany was presumably responsible for the success of the latter. The existence of only one confession in the Scandinavian lands made of Lutheranism not merely a national church but also a national religion in a more intimate sense than was possible in confessionally divided Germany. Yet despite the closeness of the union of church and state, the church retained a large measure of independence because the monarch was never as in England the head of the church. The principle of the Peace of Augsburg that the religion of a given territory might be determined by the ruler was reversed in Sweden, where the faith was imposed upon the rulers by the people. When the ultimate settlement was achieved in 1593, the nominal king was a

Roman Catholic and the regent a Calvinist, but the people achieved the adoption of the Augsburg Confession.

The stages whereby the Scandinavian settlement came to pass are complicated by the tenuousness of the union of Denmark and Sweden and Norway under a single crown. In Sweden the emancipation from Rome came to be associated with the struggle for independence against Denmark. In the 1520's the King of Denmark was Christian II, a Renaissance despot quite capable of flirting with Protestantism and of persecuting heresy according to Catholic definitions. He was a patron of learning and a vindicator of the masses. He was also an expansionist determined to make himself supreme in Sweden. The movement of opposition there was crushed and Christian then sought to secure himself by treachery. Some eighty of the opposition were promised amnesty, invited to a banquet, then hastily tried and executed on the ground of heresy. The blood bath of Stockholm in 1520 occasioned such intense resentment that in consequence Christian forfeited all control over Sweden, where the native Gustavus Vasa assumed the crown. Inasmuch as the purge had been ostensibly on the ground of heresy, even though some bishops were among the victims, Swedish opposition to the Church was intensified. Apart from this, however, Gustavus would unquestionably have sought to finance the state as he did by the spoliation of ecclesiastical goods. Coincidently Lutheran preachers were admitted, notably two brothers, Olaf and Lorenz Petri. The former anticipated Luther in the practice of clerical marriage, the latter followed in his steps by producing a Swedish translation of the Scriptures in 1526. The crisis came in 1527, which may be taken as the date of the establishment of the national church. Ecclesiastical property was vested in the king. The monasteries, despoiled of their revenues, decayed. The king might veto the decisions of high ecclesiastics and though he did not appoint them he might remove them. Reformation preaching was allowed and nothing but the pure gospel was to be taught in the schools, but episcopacy was not abolished. The transition was gradual and without violence. Sweden was not formally Lutheran until 1593.

In Denmark curiously that very Christian II who had massacred the Swedish rebels on the charge of heresy was at that very time inviting Lutheran preachers to his land. Carlstadt came from Wittenberg for a brief period. Christian proceeded rapidly in the direction of the nationalization of the Church, but a rebellion in 1523 drove him into exile. His successor, Frederick I, came in with a pledge to support the Catholic Church, but speedily began to quarrel with the pope and to tolerate the sectaries. In 1526 he consented to the marriage of his daughter with Albert of Brandenburg, former Grand Master of the Teutonic Knights, who had secularized his domains and had become the first Duke of Prussia. To take him as a husband was as bad as marrying a renegade monk. Increasingly the king declared himself not in favor of one party or another but of freedom in religion for all. The result was such an expansion of Lutheranism that in 1533, the year of the king's death, the Catholics were demanding religious liberty. Under his successor, Christian III, in 1536 came the erection of another Protestant national church. Norway became an appanage of Denmark and therefore shared in the ecclesiastical settlement.

Similarly Finland was a dependency of Sweden and became Lutheran simultaneously. The country was so culturally retarded that the first great Finnish reformer, Martin

Agricola, had not only to create a literature but also to train the people to read it. In all of the northern countries the Reformation was a great cultural force.

Inasmuch as the outcome in Sweden and Denmark was the same, the coincidence in Sweden of the Reform with the struggle for national independence must be regarded as inconsequential. With or without Protestantism the force of nationalism was so strong that Rome was due to be despoiled of wealth and power even though obedience in spirituals were retained. As a matter of fact, much of Catholic piety survived in the Scandinavian lands. The church service continued to be called the Mass. At the same time the ground tone was Lutheran. Nowhere does this better appear than in the statement of Martin Agricola: "Though my sins were as great and as many as the hairs on the head, the grass on the earth, the leaves on the trees, the sand on the shore, the drops in the sea, or the stars in heaven, yet would I not fall into despair but would betake me to the great indulgence chest, namely to the grace and overwhelming mercy of God."

9

The Fight for Recognition
of the Calvinist Faith

THE STRUGGLE OF CALVINISM for recognition took place for
the most part on a different terrain from that of the Lutheran
groups. Though the Reformed faith did eventually penetrate
the Palatinate and Württemberg, the primary areas were
France, the Netherlands, Spain, and England. In all of these
lands, however divergent the political situation, the problem
was essentially the old one — whether the ancient system of
one land and one church could be abandoned without social
chaos.

For Calvinism beyond Geneva the first land in which that
problem was posed was France. Here the whole trend was
in the direction of centralization. Nationalism had had its
earliest beginnings in France. Territories had been brought
under a central control until the boundaries were rounded
out to the natural frontiers of race, language, and geographical contours. A sturdy independence was maintained alike
toward the Empire and the papacy. At this point the medieval unity was rent in the interests of a strong internal administration. Was this process of political consolidation

compatible with the ecclesiastical fissure? The Calvinists, called in France Huguenots (why is not known), were ready to accept the ancient pattern if their faith could be substituted for that of Rome. Failing this they demanded religious liberty for themselves without perceiving that they were introducing a religious pluralism in the midst of a political monism. They were driven to inquire whether religious liberty for themselves could be squared with those absolutist tendencies toward which the state was moving; and if not, whether the state would be permitted to move in this direction. The answers given by the Calvinists to these questions will be more fully developed on the theoretical side later. This chapter will deal rather with the course of events.

The policy to be pursued by the Calvinists was conditioned by the attitude of the ruling powers and the history of the struggle in France invariably takes its outline from the succession of the kings. Generally speaking their concern was for the monarchy and for France. No one of them was deeply religious. Even those who most fiercely persecuted the innovators did so less out of religious fanaticism than from the conviction that the system of one religion was alone compatible with the stability of France. And when at last it became apparent that the attempt to enforce one religion was precisely the impediment to stability, then they were ready to espouse toleration. This attitude, which placed the interests of France above the triumph of a particular confession, is called Politique. As the monarchs veered for or against the Reform, the Calvinists became either loyalist or revolutionary.

A genealogical table of the French monarchs is of convenience in following the course of the struggle:

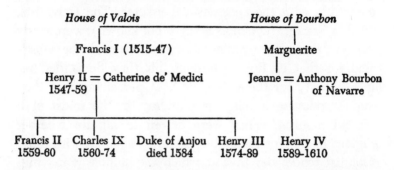

Under Francis I, as previously noted, the religious situation in France was inchoate and the lines were not sharply drawn between the Catholic evangelism of an Erasmian flavor, such as flourished coincidently in Spain and Italy, and the evangelicalism emanating from Germany. But by the 1550's the advocates of free inquiry had become suspect and in the meantime the complexion of French Protestantism was deriving its color from her own exiles who had had the good fortune to possess themselves of a citadel at Geneva. Here was an asylum for the persecuted if they could reach the border; here was a seminary for the training of missionaries to Catholic lands; here was the source of comfort and courage as John Calvin addressed his letters to princes, to nobles, and to martyrs. The aspiration of Calvinism was to convert all France, or at least to achieve recognition for itself and a sphere for wider operations.

Any such development the French monarchy under Henry II was definitely determined to impede. The vacillations of Francis I were replaced by an implacability worthy of Philip II of Spain. Every agency was employed for the prosecution of heresy: the local clergy, the Inquisition, and the secular courts, notably the Parlement at Paris. The word *parlement* in French, by the way, means not parliament but

EXECUTION OF DUBOURG

a court. To handle the volume of cases a special tribunal was created which because of the number of burnings decreed came popularly to be known as *La Chambre Ardente*, the burning chamber. During the first three years there were five hundred arrests. The king summoned to a meeting of the court those members of the ministry suspected of Lutheran sympathies and invited them to state their case. Anne de Bourg had the fortitude to declare that his faith rested on Scripture and Scripture must be the judge. So far as he could discover the teachings of the Lutherans were conformable to Scripture and those of the pope rested on human invention. He was to expiate this speech at the stake. The king derived a sadistic delight from witnessing executions. On the occasion of his entry into Paris in 1549 a resplendent procession was staged with the president of the Parlement of Paris at the head, marching in robes and scarlet hoods behind the relic of the crown of thorns from the Church of Sainte Chapelle. The king and the high dignitaries of the realm joined the procession and all attended Mass at Notre Dame. After a banquet at the episcopal residence came a tour of the executions. Some six or seven were burned that day. One was the king's tailor, who, seeing His Majesty, so fastened his eye upon him in reproach that the king for several nights could not dispel the specter, but he was not thereby deterred from witnessing fresh executions. His death from a wound received in a tournament left the orthodox inflamed and the unorthodox infuriated.

Under his son Francis II the alignment of parties became clear. The struggle centered among the nobility with one faction passionately Catholic, the other unflinchingly Protestant, and the crown caught between the two, disposed to maintain itself by playing the one against the other. The

THE FIGHT FOR RECOGNITION OF THE CALVINIST FAITH   165

Catholic party was headed by the House of Guise. Its representatives were Duke Francis of Guise who commanded the
military forces of France; his brother the Cardinal of Lorraine who presided over the finances; their sister Mary who
was married to the King of Scotland; and her daughter, their
niece, also Mary, later Mary Queen of Scots but at that time
the Queen of France. This family was ardently convinced
that the security of France rested on the maintenance of the
Catholic faith. Duke Francis on his death bed declared that
he paid no attention to any man's religion because every
man is master of his own conscience. But when he saw that
this new religion brought with it sedition and rebellion
conspiring to alter the government and the laws, he could
not watch with indifference. The Guises were perfectly prepared, if need be, even to set aside the succession and make
themselves the masters of France in order to prevent a
Protestant from coming to the throne. They were quite
willing also to call in foreign help, mercenaries whether from
Germany or from Spain.

Such readiness to supplant the ruling house and dismem-
ber France enabled the Huguenots to pose as patriots and
loyalists commissioned to deliver the king from the domination of a faction. As a matter of fact, however, the Huguenots even more than the Guises gave first place to the
religious issue and were ready in their turn to seek help
from the Schmalkaldic League, from the King of Sweden,
or from England, and even placed Le Havre in the hands
of Elizabeth in return for help. Grave searching of heart
accompanied any such recourse, and armed resistance of
any sort was a matter of concern. For some thirty years
French Calvinism was nonresistant. One of the pastors
wrote to Calvin that God can fructify the ashes of his

servants, but excesses and violence end solely in sterility.

But if the king were beguiled by a faction, should nothing be done? Calvin was disposed to feel that action could be justified if it were undertaken by the princes of the blood next in line to the succession to the throne. Resistance on their part fitted the formula that inferior magistrates might restrain the higher. The man who occupied this position was Anthony of Navarre of the House of Bourbon. His wife Jeanne was the daughter of Marguerite, the sister of Francis I. Now Marguerite had belonged to the circle of early Erasmian reformers and more than once had intervened to save a victim of repression. Her daughter Jeanne was an upright convert to Calvinism and her court at Navarre had sheltered many of the fugitives. She was not averse to seeing her husband the head of the Huguenot party, but he was vain and vacillating and easily bribed into neutrality. If then the channels of legitimacy were closed, Calvin would not countenance rebellion.

Neither at first would the most outstanding among the nobility of France, the heads of the House of Chatillon, Gaspard de Coligny and his brother Andelot. Men of conviction were they, matured on the *Institutes* of John Calvin. Their very portraits show the clear-cut, open faces of men of integrity. At this time they were restrained by their scruples from supporting the first military venture of resistance on the part of the Huguenots, the conspiracy of Amboise designed to eliminate the Guises, which ended instead in scaffolds for the conspirators. Calvin saw here only a judgment of God. Better were it in his opinion that the Reform should fail a thousand times than that it should succeed by such means. But the heads of the House of Chatillon began to wonder whether the time might not have come for an attack, since the Guises had introduced five thousand mercenaries from Lorraine and were expecting two thousand more from Germany in order to eliminate the rival House of Bourbon, even though innocent of the plot. These plans were arrested only by the sudden death of the king.

He was succeeded by his brother, Charles IX, a minor At this point begins the influence of the Queen Regent, Catherine de' Medici. If she was not quite the monster of cruelty and perfidy of the Huguenot portrayals, she was a disciple of that fellow Italian, Machiavelli, who had dedicated his work on political theory to her father. Her concern was for her house, her adopted country, and not least for herself, for she relished the power denied to her during the reigns of her husband and her elder son. Catherine desired peace within and without. She sought to avert the imminent civil war between the rival factions now allied with rival houses of the nobility. She desired also to avoid war with Spain or England. To these ends she endeavored to pit the confessions and the houses against each other. She was a Politique. Possibly she might have succeeded if she had comprehended the meaning of integrity.

Her first move was an effort to avert the imminent conflict by a reconciliation, and to that end she called the Colloquy of Poissy. For the Calvinists, Theodore Beza was given unrestricted opportunity to state the Protestant case. In so doing he not only failed to conciliate the Catholics but succeeded also in alienating the Lutherans by stating in the baldest terms the Calvinist doctrine of spiritual communion only in the Lord's Supper, seeing that the body of Christ is as far from the bread and wine as heaven from earth. Agreement on any such basis was of course out of the ques-

CARTOON AGAINST THE CALVINIST LORD'S SUPPER

A Lutheran cartoonist portrays a Calvinist minister celebrating the Lord's Supper, beneath the caption "Take, eat only in remembrance." A devil blows bellows in his ear. The legend above says that the devil perverts the world by rationalism. Christ in the upper right corner is shown chained to God's throne, a jibe at the Calvinist contention that Christ being in heaven could not be in the elements. In the lower right corner, the brazen serpent in the wilderness symbolizes Christ.

tion. Undeterred, Catherine pushed for a policy of toleration and secured the Edict of January, 1562, whereby the Huguenots were permitted freedom of public worship beyond walled towns and of private assembly within. Calvinism had thus achieved in France a limited recognition.

Yet this was to be the beginning of the wars of religion. All too truly an English observer wrote home the previous month saying, "Here is new fire, new green wood reeking, new smoke and much contrary wind blowing." He was aware that the Reform had a great hold among the feudal nobility, the gentleman farmers, and in the municipalities. The artisans in general were Huguenot, the peasants Catholic. Calvinism had a real chance to become the religion of France, and this the Guises would not tamely suffer. They were not willing to concede the liberties accorded to the innovators by the Edict of January. When the Duke of Guise with an armed escort came upon some Huguenots worshiping in a barn, he ordered them to leave and they answered with cries of "papist and idolator." Stones flew. The duke's armed retainers fired and killed 63 out of six or seven hundred worshipers. This set off the wars. Coligny and Andelot confronted the Guises. The Huguenots, who had hitherto been restrained, had recourse also to violence, not through massacre but through the desecration of the sacrament and the demolition of churches and images.

Three wars followed with no conclusive termination. The peace at the end of each reaffirmed something close to the Edict of January. Ten years went by from 1562 to 1572 with desultory fighting and the multiplying of atrocities on both sides. The men of moderation lifted their heads. How long could this go on? Should France be rent by mercenaries from Germany and mercenaries from Spain? Should she be bled in fratricidal conflict in order in the end that Spain should profit from her plight? Even one of the bishops issued an appeal in which he said, "If I say to a Catholic 'Of what religion were you six months ago?' he answers 'I was of the Catholic religion.' Then I say to him, 'Do you call that religion Catholic which permits the violation of public faith, the exciting of seditions, the pillaging and strangling of brothers?' And if the same question were addressed to one of the Reformed and he admitted his adherence, I would say, 'What abominable reform has authorized you to overturn altars, profane sacred vessels, and commit the most revolting excesses against persons conse-

crated to God? Both of you should give up names which
do not befit you, because the Christian religion has nothing
in common with the profession of brigands.' "

Catherine de' Medici, profiting by the revulsion of feeling
against violence and inconclusive wars, came forward with
a plan of reconciliation. The two confessions as well as
the two royal houses of Valois and Bourbon should be ce-
mented in a marriage between Catherine's daughter and
Henry of Navarre. The latter had been reared as a Huguenot
by his mother Jeanne and was still of that faith; though
he was far from being a man of profound conviction, at least
he was a Huguenot. Better still the Guises and the Chatillons
were invited to Paris for the wedding. But a gesture of
reconciliation on the part of the queen served only to set off
the renewal of conflict. The religious issue had come to
be complicated by a private feud. In the previous wars
Duke Francis of Guise had been assassinated by a Huguenot,
and Coligny was believed by Duke Henry, the son and successor of the murdered duke, to have been privy to the
plot. Apart from this Catherine herself was growing jealous
of Coligny because of his ascendancy over her son Charles
IX and she disapproved also of Coligny's prescription for
unifying France through a war with Spain. At the time of
the wedding festivities the Guises attempted the assassination of Coligny and failed. Catherine took fright, decided
that the coup having been attempted would have to be
finished, and could not now be finished by killing Coligny
alone since his followers had been alerted. They too must
be exterminated. Charles IX consented. The Massacre of
St. Bartholomew followed on August 23, 1572. Contemporaries estimated that ten thousand fell in Paris and similar

massacres followed in the provinces. The pope struck a medal in honor of the event.

Every such act of violence caused revulsion. The south of France in the province of Languedoc was won for the policy of the Politique and conceivably their program might earlier have been achieved had it not been that the death of the Duke of Anjou in 1584 made Henry of Navarre, the Huguenot, the heir to the throne. This succession the Guises would not tolerate and to prevent it they precipitated a series of wars called the Wars of the Three Henrys, from Henry of Guise, Henry of Valois the King, and Henry of Navarre. The first move of the Guises was an attempt to seize the person of the king. He eluded them and countered by murdering the Duke of Guise.

This atrocity revolted even the more moderate Catholics and Henry III, the king, had in consequence to align himself with the Protestants under Henry of Navarre. Together the two remaining Henrys, the Valois and the Bourbon, marched on Paris. While they were laying siege to the city an agent of the sister of the murdered Duke of Guise insinuated himself into the camp of the besiegers and assassinated the king. Henry of Navarre was then left in the direct line of succession to the throne, but the Catholics would not suffer him to enter into his inheritance because of his religion. For fully a decade he endeavored to take Paris. Catholic resistance from within and Spanish intervention from without by way of the Netherlands impeded him. At length he decided to achieve by a change of religion what he could not accomplish by force of arms. He made his submission to Rome with a touch of levity inasmuch as religion had never meant to him what it did to his mother. He, too, was a

Politique, and his concern was primarily for France. The support which he could now enlist from the south firmly entrenched him in his position.

He had brought peace to France and he hastened to solve the religious difficulty by an edict which made Calvinism in France, like Lutheranism in Germany, a tolerated religion. The Edict of Nantes in 1598 guaranteed that no man should be molested because of his faith. Private worship was permissible anywhere. Public worship was allowed in designated places including the estates of some three thousand nobles. The Huguenots were given full civil rights, permission to enter universities, schools and hospitals, and to hold all public offices. They received representation on judicial tribunals and were to enjoy full liberty for church assemblies. They might even discuss political questions on permission from the king. In order to guarantee the observance of these concessions the Huguenots were granted control of two hundred fortified towns. This proved to have been a mistake because the Protestants became thereby a state within the state and a potential menace to national unity.

The Edict of Nantes was in force for only eighty-seven years. In 1685 the French monarchy reached the peak of absolutism and Louis XIV eliminated the threat of ecclesiastical pluralism by returning to *une foi, un roi, une loi*. His successors were to expiate his intransigence on the guillotine.

In the Low Countries the struggle of Protestantism for recognition coincided with a war of liberation against Spain. Charles V had contrived, while outraging Protestants, to retain the affection of Catholics in the Netherlands and they constituted the majority of the population. He had been reared in the Low Countries and would sometimes abet them

even against the interests of the Empire. There were tears
at Brussels when he abdicated in 1555. His son Philip II
was very different, not speaking Flemish like his father but
only Spanish, and interested merely in manipulating the
Netherlands as a tool of Spanish policy. By exorbitant taxa-
tion, the quartering of Spanish troops and the appointment
of Spanish officials, he alienated even those who were not
incensed by the introduction of the Spanish Inquisition.
So intense was the resentment that at moments the entire
country could be enlisted for resistance. The spirit of the
opposition was always Calvinist.

The religious situation in the Low Countries was, however, more mixed than anywhere save in Poland and the
lands to the east. The reason was probably that countries
not yet subject to a high degree of political centralization
exercised in general less constant restraints upon dissent of
any sort, and were therefore congenial to religious diversity.
Long before the Reformation Holland had had a tradition in
this respect: it was Erasmian before Erasmus. In fact
Erasmus was Erasmian because he was Dutch. The Brethren
of the Common Life among whom he was trained had long
cultivated a Biblical humanism. Holland was the home of
sacramentarianism. Here flourished Cornelius Hoen, whose
interpretation of the Lord's Supper in symbolic terms had
determined the view of Zwingli. One is not surprised in
the light of this background to find Holland in the 1530's
the greatest center of the Anabaptist movement.

In the meantime came the infiltration of Lutheranism.
The Marrani, converted Jews from Spain, engaged in commerce at Antwerp, were hospitable to Luther's teaching.
Here first his books were burned and the earliest Lutheran
martyrs were in the Low Countries. Around the 1560's came

the great Calvinist inroad which was ultimately to dominate the northern provinces. There were, then, when Philip II succeeded to the throne, at least three major bodies in the Low Countries: the Catholics, the Lutherans, and the Calvinists. And although thousands of Anabaptists had been executed or expelled, a sufficient residue remained to constitute a smaller fourth party. The presence of so many bodies in such strength meant that the problem of toleration was much more complicated than in those countries where the Catholic Church was confronted by not more than one rival. One of the greatest obstacles to a solution was the intolerance of the Protestant bodies toward each other. On one occasion the Lutherans stood in arms together with the Catholics in order to restrain the Calvinists.

Why Calvinism in the end should have gained the ascendancy among the Protestant bodies is a matter of speculation. The proximity of Germany to the northern provinces might have given the lead to Lutheranism. On the other hand, Calvinism was sufficiently aggressive to make headway even in Germany and obtained a footing in the Palatinate where the standard Calvinist profession of faith, the Heidelberg Catechism, was issued. Also in Germany proper, in Württemberg, Calvinism gained a hold. The success in the Netherlands may well have been due to the fact that Calvinism was better suited to be the religion of a resistance movement. The activism of the Calvinists, their progress in France in divesting themselves of all of the earlier scruples with regard to the legitimacy of armed resistance to tyranny, their heroic devotion to the glory of God by erecting His kingdom upon earth made them just the group to drive "the Spanish vermin from the land."

This particular expression came from William of Orange

who was to be the leader of the great rebellion. Oddly enough he had been the favorite of the Emperor Charles V and supported his arm on the occasion of his abdication. But William had been disillusioned while held as a hostage at the court of France. There Henry II one day inadvertently disclosed to him the secret clauses of the treaty between France and Spain for the extirpation of heresy in their respective domains, including of course the Netherlands. William, perceiving that the king had supposed him to be already acquainted with the treaty, held his peace, and for that reason came to be known as William the Silent though as a matter of fact he was eloquent in half a dozen tongues. And then it was that he resolved to drive the Spanish vermin from the land.

He could count on Protestant help provided the confessions did not devour each other. After the frightful barbarities of Philip II and the Duke of Alva, there were moments when the support of the entire populace could be assumed. But even so, a little country like the Netherlands could scarcely expect to throw off the yoke of Spain apart from help from the outside, and William negotiated with the German Lutherans, who would render no assistance unless the Calvinists would sign the Augsburg Confession. He negotiated with England, and Elizabeth harbored the so-called Sea Beggars, essentially pirates flying the flag of William. He turned to France, and Coligny was only too eager to solve his country's internal problems by a foreign war and to expel the Spanish vermin. But that was just what Catherine de' Medici did not want. Coligny's ambition in this regard was one of the reasons for the attempted assassination and for the massacre of St. Batholomew, and this in turn ended all hope of help from France. William found himself in sore straits, but when reminded that he could not succeed without the help of some potentate, he answered, "When I undertook the defense of these oppressed Christians I made an alliance with the mightiest of all potentates, the Lord of Hosts, who is able to save us if He choose."

Whether or no William could succeed depended in part on whether he could enlist and maintain the united support of all the people. To do so he needed to be able to offer a solution of the religious problem. His own position appeared to many of his contemporaries to be quite as Politique as that of Henry IV, except that he moved in the opposite direction. William was in turn a Catholic, a Lutheran, and a Calvinist. The changes were presumably in a measure opportunist. He was a man of very profound religious faith, but not interested in confessional niceties. At this point he was an heir of the Erasmian tradition. Calvinism may have appealed to him because it had come so strongly to countenance the doctrine that lower magistrates might defend the liberties and the consciences of the people against the higher. William justified his own assumption of revolutionary leadership on the ground that he was a prince of the blood, Burggraaf of Antwerp, member of the estates of Brabant, Stadhouder of Holland and Zeeland, and Knight of the Golden Fleece.

But however much he might be authorized, there was still the problem of how the religious difficulty was to be solved. He was ready to experiment. At one time he suggested extension of the territorial principle to such minute lengths that each town would have a quarter for each religion, Catholic, Lutheran, Calvinist, and Mennonite, not to mention the Jews. It would be like setting up five ghettos. This of course was never tried. On another occasion he succeeded in enacting into law an edict of complete toleration. The Peace of Antwerp in 1578 accorded full liberty. "Touching religion each should be free as he would have to answer to God." The Catholics should be tolerated in Protestant lands as the Protestants should be tolerated also in the Catholic. But this arrangement was short-lived, terminated by the intolerance of both sides.

In the end it became apparent that only the territorial solution was feasible. The Low Countries, like Switzerland, were a conglomeration which the religious issue once more split open. The Swiss fortunately were not actually occupied by the Hapsburgs and were able to work out their territorial division without disrupting the political unity of the Confederation. The Netherlands did not succeed. The northern provinces of Holland and Zeeland spoke Dutch; in their cultural life they were closer to Germany and England. They had come to be prevailingly Calvinist. The southern provinces of Brabant and Flanders spoke French and Flemish; they were closer culturally to France. In the south the privileged conservative classes, the nobility and the higher ecclesiastics, were stronger. In the north the enterprising merchants took the lead. Besides, the north with its islands and dykes was easier to defend. All of these considerations pointed to that division which eventuated in the creation of Belgium and Holland. The year 1581 saw the declaration of the independence of the Dutch Republic. The religious division carried with it a certain exchange of populations.

In Belgium, Catholicism remained the established religion, and there was no further talk of religious liberty until the Edict of Joseph II was reluctantly accepted in 1781. In Holland Calvinism was established and in a very

vigorous form. Relaxation came later less by positive repeal
of enactments than by the actual mitigation of penalties.

The other area of Europe in which Calvinism gained a
hold was in the East, in Poland, where the field was shared
with Catholics, Lutherans, Hussites, Socinians and Anabaptists. There, as already noted, three groups in 1573 agreed
to recognize each other, namely the Lutherans, the Calvinists, and the Hussites. But their accord soon succumbed to
Catholic attack. In Hungary and Transylvania, Calvinism
likewise penetrated along with Anabaptism and Socinianism.
All fared better under the Turks than under the Hapsburgs.
Of these three Calvinism alone survives, presumably because less radical in doctrine and social ethics, but perhaps
also because readier to have recourse to armed resistance.

Scotland was the land in Europe above all others in
which Calvinism became most firmly entrenched. Even in
Holland the Calvinists were challenged by the Arminians,
Remonstrants, and to a degree by the Mennonites. Scotland's rifts were family quarrels among Calvinists, and in
no other land did Calvinism effect so tremendous a change
in the national character and the national destiny. Calvinism
transformed the Scots. In the Middle Ages they were a
notoriously rough and disorderly people who preferred to
raid rather than to raise cattle. A Scotch bard related that
once Christ and St. Peter were walking in the land of
Argyle when Peter suggested that the Lord create a Highlander out of a horse turd. As he uprose the Lord said to him,

"Where wilt thou now?"
"I will doun in the Lawland, Lord, and there steal a cow!"
"And thou steal a cow, carle, there they will hang thee."
"What reck, Lord, of that for anis [once] mon I die."

Immediately thereafter Christ missed his dagger. (What he was doing with it in the first place is another matter.) The Highlander turned around and it fell out of his plaid. St. Peter reproached him.

"Fy," quod Saint Peter, "thou will never do weill:
  And thou bot new made and sa soon gais [goes] to steal."
"Humf," quod the Hielandman, and sware by yon kirk,
"Sa lang as I may gear get to steal, I will never wirk."

The Reformation changed all that. The Scots were to become a different people and the alteration was effected by the new kirk armed with the Book of Discipline.

For the political fortunes of the Scots the Reformation was no less momentous. Without it they could never have been joined to England — unless of course England had reverted to Catholicism. In that period a political consolidation was inconceivable if there were a major difference in religion. Either both countries must be Catholic or both Protestant. By the same token the diversity in Protestantism between Presbyterianism and Anglicanism was an important factor in England's later civil wars. The principle that one territory should and could have one religion was still so strong that the English sought to enforce the Prayer Book on the Scots and the Scots to impose the Westminster Confession upon the English. The character of the Puritan struggle was conditioned in part by the differences between the two ecclesiastical systems. The Scots along with the rest of Europe centered the essence of religion in a confession, the English in a book of worship. In theology proper there was little quarrel because the English were not insistent upon theology. Polity and liturgy became the areas of conflict.

The Reformation in Scotland is associated with the name of one man, John Knox. That of itself is not incredible when one recalls the influence of a Luther and a Calvin. What is puzzling is that Knox should have played so exclusive a role *in absentia,* for until 1559 he was repeatedly away from Scotland. He took over at the moment when the Mass had been decreed a penal offense. His decisive part belongs to the second phase of the revolution when the movement was imperiled by a counterattack. The initial phases of the Reformation were compounded of popular disaffection against clerical abuses peculiarly prevalent in so disorderly a land, recurring periods of pro-English and anti-French feeling especially acute when Mary Stuart's position as Queen of France threatened to make of Scotland a French dependency, and genuine evangelical preaching conducted by reformers who proclaimed the gospel without regard to worldly fortunes. In the period of Edward VI, English Bibles were sent to Scotland by cartloads, and popular ballads attacking the church and celebrating the new faith were more extensive than in England. A contemporary observed with some amazement that in England whereas the government favored the Reformation the people were "contumacious"; in Scotland, on the contrary, "the rulers are most ferocious, but the nation at large is virtuous and exceedingly well disposed towards our most holy religion."

The man who gave shape to the revolutionary temper was John Knox. He was one of the most implacable of all the reformers. If he is not to be written off simply as a blustering fanatic, first it must be remembered that he emerged in a day when the last vestige of mellowness had faded. The year 1560 was indeed prior to St. Bartholomew's, but it was after the Roman Inquisition, the Schmalkaldic

War, the opening sessions of the Council of Trent, and the foundation of the Jesuits. And John Knox had had a rough indoctrination. He was first drawn to public participation in the Reformation by the execution of the reformer Wishart, and his first actual post was as chaplain to the besieged band responsible for the assassination of the representative alike of Rome and France and Scotland — Cardinal Beaton. The arrival of a French fleet meant for Knox a year as a galley slave with physical debility and frequent bullying to adore the Virgin. He saw continental Catholicism in the raw. Released, he was given a post in England under Edward VI when the Reform in that land was assuming more and more radical aspects. On the accession of Mary he was allowed to escape to the Continent to receive a further grounding at Geneva and Zurich. There he was inducted into the staggering Calvinist plan of the ages according to which God, through the elect, should rear His kingdom upon earth. Knox, hardened by personal indignities and the news of former colleagues burned at the stake, was more intransigent than the continentals and less inhibited than they in espousing the doctrine of revolution against rulers who impede the will of God. Knox felt toward the idolators as Elijah toward the priests of Baal, and in his eyes the Mass, a ceremony instituted without the warrant of the Word of God, was idolatry and likewise blasphemy since it was an encroachment upon the sole sacrifice of Christ. A single celebration of the Mass appeared to him therefore worse than taking a cup of poison.

In this mood Knox came into Scotland to assume the leadership of an already covenanted Band. And in the same year Mary Stuart, through the death of her husband no longer Queen of France, came home to be Queen of Scots and had Mass celebrated in her private chapel. The ensuing altercation between the pretty girl and the tirading reformer evokes no sympathy for Knox in an age which has forgotten what it was all about. For him not only was the Mass poison but the queen's Mass was the insidious prelude to an overthrow of the solemn league and the establishment of a regime like that of Bloody Mary with the fires of Smithfield. The incredible follies, not to say misdemeanors, of the queen led to her flight to England, where for years she remained a prisoner until implication in plots on the life of Elizabeth ended in her execution.

In the meantime Knox had made of the Scotch a Calvinist nation in so far as that could be done without expelling all dissidents and bringing in outside reinforcements as at Geneva. This Scotland never did. The pattern was rather one of minority domination, not by dragonnades but by the power of disciplined example. The church itself was built around the communion table to which only those rigorously tested were admitted. The outreach of the church on the community was facilitated by the unparalleled development of the lay leadership, and the influence exerted on the national life through the General Assembly which could as little be flouted by the king as could Parliament. Scotch and Presbyterian have never since been dissociated.

10

Comprehension and the Middle Way of Anglicanism

THE THIRD GREAT SOLUTION of the problem of religious liberty, the way of comprehension, found its most perfect exemplification in the age of the Reformation in England. This method, as already indicated, is territorial in that the persons to be comprehended are the inhabitants of a given political domain. But the point is not to maintain rigidly the integrity of the particular confession, no matter how many are alienated, but rather to comprise as many as possible in a single church by making minimal and ambiguous demands. Territorialism stresses truth at the expense of unity, and comprehension stresses unity at the expense if not of truth at least of clarity. The situation is paralleled when any one group essays a pronouncement on a controverted question. The issues will most sharply emerge if there be a majority and also a minority report. If there be but a single document, the statements are bound to be guarded, noncommittal and perhaps blurred.

The reason why England in the sixteenth century was amenable to such a solution was that in this period the land was not passionately stirred over confessional issues. Not until the Puritan revolution in the next century was the pattern of Luther's Germany or Coligny's France reproduced in England. From this land emanated no distinctive confession and no great work on theology. The most outstanding literary product of the Anglican Reformation was Richard Hooker's *Laws of Ecclesiastical Polity*, and it dealt not with theology but with church government. The theology of Anglicanism was a conglomerate and with pride was called "The Middle Way."

The rhythm of English life at the moment demanded tranquillity. There had been disturbance enough in the earlier period through sectarianism and heresy in Wyclif and the Lollards, and more than enough disorder in the political sphere in the Wars of the Roses. England wanted above all else security and order, and these were best afforded through the new nationalism which sought to ensure each sovereign state from inner dissension and outer interference. The pope was one of the exterior and interfering powers that the new national states — Spain, France, and England — had for some time been seeking to curb, albeit without open rupture. In Spain the Inquisition had been turned into an instrument of state, even despite papal protest. In France, Gallicanism effectually controlled the exportation of gold to Rome, appeals to Rome, and appointments by Rome. In England the figure of Wolsey is a symbol of the degree to which independence had been achieved prior to the schism. He combined in his own person the Church in England, the Church of Rome, and the Kingdom of England — for he was the Archbishop of York, a cardinal and legate of the pope, and chancellor of the realm. And all this he was as the king's henchman subject to appointment, elevation, or recall at the royal whim. The nationalizing of churches was thus possible to a very large degree apart from schism.

This degree of independence might have sufficed for England if the papacy had retained its character as a genuinely international institution impartial in its dealings with the rival national states; but such was not the case, because the Vatican at the beginning of the second quarter of the century succumbed to the control of Spain. Charles V of the Holy Roman Empire renewed the medieval strife between the two heads of Christendom, with the result that in 1527 Rome was sacked by the imperial troops and the pope became the prisoner of the emperor, and though subsequently released was still under his domination. Now Charles was himself in an anomalous position, both international as emperor and national as king of Spain. Under the circumstances then, for the pope to be worsted by the emperor meant actually to be dominated by Spain. In such a case should England then submit to the pope at points where any subservience to Spain might contravene national interests? A similar position a century and a half earlier had almost resulted in schism. At that time France controlled the papacy in residence at Avignon. The emperor Louis of Bavaria became restive, rebelled, and was long under an interdict, and in England the heretic Wyclif was suffered to die in bed because English sovereigns would not heed the thunders of Avignonese popes. Had not the papacy returned to Rome, Germany and England, not to mention Spain, might easily have withdrawn obedience. In the days of Henry VIII, Spain was dominant and therefore not restive. France was planted on Gallicanism. Germany was already rent by the Reformation. England's case was not precisely that of any of the others.

The immediate occasion of the Anglican quarrel was an attempt to annul a royal marriage. If there was to be a rift with Rome, it was almost bound to occur at the point of matrimony because so much else was already cared for. Judicial and financial encroachments had been so curtailed that England could not like Germany be appropriately dubbed "the pope's private cow." But so long as marriage remained a sacrament of the Church, and so long as the authority of the Church was not rejected, ecclesiastical jurisdiction at this point could not very well be denied. The problem of Henry VIII was not passion but succession. He knew how to satisfy passion without benefit of matrimony and already had an illegitimate son — but not one to succeed him born of the queen, and no hope of one after 1525, for although in that year Henry was but thirty-three, his wife Katherine was forty. Five of her children had arrived stillborn or had died within a few months. The only survivor was the princess Mary; she was a girl and for that reason regarded as no solution by an England whose only previous queen had occasioned wars of succession. The repetition of such a calamity in a land already blanched by the Wars of the Roses was at all costs to be avoided. The popularity of the Tudors rested on their success in terminating the anarchy, and now should all this be jettisoned because the queen could not supply an heir? Divorce in the proper sense of the term was inadmissible, but an annulment might be possible if some flaw could be discovered invalidating the marriage from the outset. In this instance it was not far to seek, because Katherine had been Henry's deceased brother's wife and on such a union the book of Leviticus pronounced a curse: "If a man shall take his brother's wife it is an unclean thing. They shall be childless." (Lev. 20:21.) The difficulty, of course, had been recognized at the time of the union of Henry and Katherine, but the match at that moment seemed so imperative that a papal dispensation had been secured to cover the impediment. The situation was that the sixteen-year-old Katherine had been married to Prince Arthur at fourteen in the year 1501. In less than half a year he had died. The dowry had not yet been fully paid. Ferdinand, the father of the bride, demanded back the portion already discharged, and Henry VII, the father of the groom, insisted on the part unpaid. To validate the claim he thought that despite his age he might play David to Katherine as the Shunamite, but the better expedient presented itself of marrying her to his younger son, Henry, six years her junior. To make this possible Pope Julius II granted the dispensation. But had not the sequel of heirlessness demonstrated that the pope had overstepped himself in setting aside the curse of God, and might not the present pope reverse the predecessor by discovering some flaw in the dispensation? If one regard this plea on the part of Henry as sheer hypocrisy in view of his infatuation with Anne Boleyn, be it remembered that, when a divorce was first rumored, Anne was but seven years old. Nor was Henry necessarily insincere in believing that the Scriptural curse had blighted his marriage. Medical knowledge was not sufficiently advanced to fasten the responsibility incontestably upon his own disease.

The solution appeared simple. Let Clement VII set aside the dispensation and declare the marriage invalid from the outset. The pope was not outraged by the proposal on the score of morality, although he found it embarrassing to be asked to reverse his predecessor. He suggested bigamy as preferable. But he was perfectly ready to entertain Henry's proposal and commissioned Cardinal Wolsey and Campeggio to try the case, and moreover not at Rome but in England.

Henry had every reason to believe that the pope would be amenable — and so indeed he might have been, had not Katherine been the aunt of Charles, the king of Spain, Holy Roman Emperor and controller of the pope. His Holiness endeavored to satisfy both parties and through Campeggio proposed to Katherine that she take the veil, but Katherine would not oblige. She declined to recognize the jurisdiction of the court sitting in England, declared that her marriage with Arthur had never been consummated and that therefore no impediment ever existed. The only recourse then left to the pope was to stall, and when the postponement of judgment appeared no longer tenable Campeggio prorogued the court from July of 1529 until October on the ground that since papal courts did not sit during the hot days of the Italian summer, therefore they should not do so in England.

Henry decided to take things into his own hands. This was a problem even for a Tudor, for although the monarchy had never been so absolute yet no monarch can ever act in total disregard of popular opinion. The England of that day was marked by a coincidence of personal piety and anti-clericalism. The books printed in England as late as 1540 contained a very high proportion of Catholic manuals of devotion such as *The Traytte of god Lyvyng and Good Deyng* (1503), *The doctrynall of dethe* (1532), or *The Pilgrimage of Perfection* (1526). At the same time resentment was rife against clericalism and papalism, with very little trace, however, of any heretical tendencies which had either burned out or been burned up since the days of Wyclif. A residue of Lollardry survived, though how extensive cannot be computed. A group called Christian Brethren were intrepid in subsidizing the printing of evangelical books in English abroad and in smuggling them into the country.

The English clergy who sat among the peers might be more intractable, but if their privileges were protected against papal encroachment and their revenues not expropriated for the royal exchequer they might be compliant. Henry set to work by a tactic — since devastatingly employed by dictators — of spacing shocks and launching the second only after the first had been absorbed. Wolsey had already been deposed and he had been so overweening that none lamented his demise. The king sought next to break the spirit of the clergy as a whole, and with singular effrontery accused them of violating the antiquarian statute of *Praemunire* which forbade appeals to Rome without the king's consent. The violation consisted in recognizing Wolsey as the pope's legate though the king himself had heartily acquiesced. The clergy succumbed in silence. The ecclesiastical convocation itself agreed to forgo the right of legislation without the royal consent, and next, as a weapon with which to bludgeon the pope, Henry demanded that he be given authority at discretion to cut off papal annates. Parliament complied though the clerical members dissented.

Henry then undertook to have in readiness an ecclesiastical machinery with which to supplement Rome in case the breach should come. The Archbishop of Canterbury was the appropriate person to serve as the primate of an English national church. He must be personally pliable. When the incumbent died, the choice fell on Thomas Cranmer. He was a sincere reformer with Lutheran leanings who had first attracted attention through his suggestion in the matter of the "divorce" that not the canon lawyers but the universities should be invited to render judgment. Henry jumped at the plan, and promptly commissioned Cranmer to collect the opinions of Continental faculties. Cranmer himself

favored annulment. He was, then, the man for the archbishopric. He was consecrated by the pope, who was
cognizant of his views, and Cranmer swore allegiance to the
pope though aware that he might soon renounce him. The
principle of mental reservation covered such cases.

The last preliminary step by Henry was to secure from
Parliament an act forbidding the clergy to appeal to Rome
and requiring them to defy papal anathemas and to continue
to administer the sacraments despite excommunication and
interdict. The king was now ready. The first move in the
breach proper was the Act of Succession which declared the
marriage of Henry and Katherine annulled. Katherine henceforth should be known as the dowager of Arthur. The
king's beloved wife Anne was queen and their daughter
Elizabeth heiress — a girl after all! Any who should slander
or derogate the king's said lawful matrimony should be guilty
of high treason. The authority cited was that of Parliament
and of Thomas, Archbishop of Canterbury, metropolitan and
primate of this realm. Apparently there was to be a national
church with an ecclesiastical head. This was in the spring
of 1534, but in the November following the Act of Supremacy
declared: "The king's majesty justly and rightly is and ought
to be and shall be reputed the only supreme head in earth
of the Church of England called *Anglicana Ecclesia.*" The
clergy submitted to the king's proclamation abolishing the
"usurped jurisdiction of the Bishop of Rome."

It was done. A national church with the king at its head
had been proclaimed with a logical clarity that was never
achieved by Frenchmen or Spaniards, but only by English-
men. Something new had come into being for which there
were partial but no complete precedents. After the barbarian
invasions there had been for a time a church in England out

of touch with Rome, but it was not a national church because at that time there was no English nation. The Bohemian Hussites had had for a time a national church but they were not orthodox. Sweden a few years earlier had established a a national church, but the impetus came from the people who impressed on the crown an endorsement of Lutheranism and the king did not become the head of the church. The fullest parallel was to be found in the Caeseropapism of Justinian, a system thoroughly orthodox in which the parallelism of the ecclesiastical and the civil was solved by a demarcation of sphere in which the whole realm of action fell to imperial control.

The political theory involved in Henry's establishment will be discussed more fully in a subsequent chapter. Suffice it to point out here that there were limitations upon the king's supremacy. He was called the head of the church but he was not a priest. He might appoint but could not consecrate bishops. The ancient saying that "the purple makes emperors, not priests," had by no means been abandoned. The king might influence the formulation of dogma but he was still a layman, not the maker but only the defender of the faith. The title had been conferred on Henry by the pope as a recognition for his services in refuting Luther. Henry took it quite seriously. His rupture with Rome did not mean that the faith had been altered, and Henry may well have considered himself quite as good a champion as the frivolous popes of the Renaissance — if not better.

Only two serious changes were introduced into the life of the church in Henry's reign, and neither one affected doctrine. The first was the suppression of the monasteries. The ostensible ground was the enormities practiced by the inmates. The charges were epitomized in Simon Fish's "Supplication of Beggars," in which the monastics were described as "foul, unhappy lepers who lived only by almesse, who despoil poor wives of the tenth egg, and indulge in cucoldry." Yet the treatment accorded the expelled monks and nuns belies the charges. Had they been guilty they might well have been sent to Tyburn. Instead they were handsomely pensioned.

The real reason was incontestably financial, and the crown did reap considerable revenues from the confiscation. Only in rare instances were monastic lands conferred outright upon some nobleman as a reward for signal services. Commonly the transfer to private hands came as a result of sale. Such expropriations could scarcely be palatable to Rome yet they need not of themselves have entailed even censure, let alone schism. Had not the pope himself consented to the suppression of the order of the Templars? And Wolsey before the breach had suppressed no fewer than twenty-one monasteries in order to use their endowments for colleges at Oxford and elsewhere, and this without papal rebuke.

Henry's dissolution was of course more drastic than anything that had occurred previously because in the end he abolished all of the houses. He could scarcely have done so without provoking serious disaffection if the religious had been held in their onetime esteem. But from the days of Chaucer, English monasticism had been characterized neither by flagrant enormity nor by conspicuous saintliness and learning. The best that could be said on the latter score was that the monks had preserved — not that they had augmented — libraries. Apart from the general law of diminution of energy, there were special reasons for the decline in monastic zeal. For instance, the Black Death of 1348 had so devastated the population that to secure thereafter the proper number of dedicated inmates to man the houses became very difficult. Moreover, the role of the monasteries at the point of hospitality was in part their undoing. The traveling nobility expected not only to be sumptuously fed but also to be diverted and entertained through minstrelsy and plays performed by the monks themselves. How little sense of vocation remained was evident in Henry's day in that when he first suppressed the lesser monasteries and gave the religious the opportunity either of transferring to other houses or of entering secular walks of life, fully one half chose the latter alternative. The abbots themselves cannot have been very zealous for the Lord God of Hosts in that twenty-one of them in 1530 signed the petition to the pope to accede to Henry's desire about the divorce; and that four of them assisted at the christening of the princess Elizabeth.

No change in doctrine indeed was involved in the dissolution — yet a certain change of attitude was implicit. One of Henry's pamphleteers charged that when the monks were taxed with failing to give the prince due succor they would invariably reply:

> We are poor bedemen of Your Grace
> We pray for your deceased ancestrees
> For whom we sing masses and dirigees [dirges]
> And succor their souls in needful haste.

The primary function of the monks was to pray, and both the donor and the sovereign considered themselves sufficiently recompensed if the supplication of the religious on their behalf ascended to heaven. That Henry's propagandist should find it necessary only to state the plea to have it regarded as ridiculous betokens a new attitude.

The case was very similar with regard to the setting up of the Bible in the vernacular in the churches. Rome did not object to versions in the native tongue provided they were orthodox and authorized. The Wyclifite version was unacceptable as the work of heretics. Henry's order therefore that an English Bible be installed in all the churches would not of itself have invited papal censure. Nevertheless it is not too much to say that a genuinely scholarly translation taken directly from the Hebrew and the Greek was at that period bound to offend the Church of Rome because certain renderings of the Latin version commonly adduced in support of crucial doctrines would be expunged. There is for example the famous text which in the Latin is rendered "do penance," whereas the Greek means simply "be penitent." In England, moreover, the zeal for translation was evident only among those addicted not only to the new learning but also to the new religion.

Conspicuous among them was William Tyndale. Henry earlier in his reign had been implacably opposed to giving any countenance to the endeavors of Tyndale, who was driven with the aid of wealthy friends to live, labor, and print abroad and then to import his works into England. A curious tale is related of how he contrived to turn the devices of his foes to advantage. The Archbishop of Canterbury was buying up his translations for burning and commissioned a certain Packington to scour the continent for more. This man went straight to Tyndale himself and informed him that he had discovered a merchant who would clean out his stock.

"Who is this merchant?" said Tyndale.

"The bishop of London," said Packington.

"Oh, that is because he will burn them," said Tyndale.

"Yea, marry," quoth Packington.

"I am the gladder," said Tyndale, "for these two benefits shall come thereof: I shall get money from him for these books and bring myself out of debt, and the whole world shall cry out on the burning of God's Word, and the overplus of the money that shall remain to me shall make me more studious to correct the said New Testament, and so newly to imprint the same once again; and I trust the second will much better like you than ever did the first."

And the account concludes: "And so forward went the bargain: the bishop had the books, Packington had the thanks, and Tyndale had the money."

Henry's agents struck then not at the books but at their author. Tyndale was betrayed by a fellow countryman to the Catholic authorities in Belgium and there burned in the year 1536. Curiously the decision had in the meantime been reached to set up the Bible in English in the churches and the commission to procure them was assigned to Coverdale, who being unable to produce a translation in such short order, availed himself of Tyndale's — which became thereby the standard version and the basis for the King James. A sample passage of 287 words from the latter version has incorporated 242 of them from Tyndale. A single specimen must suffice to exhibit Tyndale's style and manifest influence: "And he spake unto his disciples, therefore I say unto you, take no thought for your life what ye shall eat, neither for your body, what ye shall put on. The life is more than meat and the body is more than raiment. Consider the ravens, for they neither sow nor reap, which neither have storehouse nor barn, and yet God feedeth them. How much more are ye better than the fowls."

Henry's program of schism without heresy provoked some disaffection both to the right and to the left. In the north there were risings occasioned in part by social grievances and in part by indignation over the suppression of the monasteries. The insurrections collapsed in no small measure because of the loyalty of the insurgents, who could not persuade themselves to go far against the Lord's anointed. Apart from these positive rebellions some of the most distinguished and noble leaders in church and state went to the block for refusal to take the oath to the king as the supreme head of the church. Among them were the saintly Cardinal Fisher and the equally saintly Sir Thomas More, onetime chancellor of the realm. Many efforts were made to break him down. Lady More visited him in prison and marveled that one of his wisdom should be content to lie in filth among mice and rats when he might enjoy his gallery and garden and the society of his family if only he would follow the example of all the bishops and the most learned of the realm. This plea was easy to reject, but that of his daughter Meg was seductive because she understood. More called her playfully his Eve. She recognized of course that her father could not go counter to his conscience. But was he after all sure of his conscience, since he conceded that others who had taken the oath might be conscientious? How could he refrain from passing judgment on them if he were sure of himself? Meg had placed her finger on a very crucial question — whether conscience can be relative and yet binding. Is it possible for men to take opposite courses of action and yet be equally sincere and scrupulous? More took his stand squarely for the absolute obligation of a relative conscience. "The high judge," said he, "might exalt others to heaven who swore in good conscience, and yet for the same consign him to the devil because he did not think as they thought." "Daughter," he concluded, "I never intend to pin my soul to another man's back." Saint Thomas More died after all for the right of private judgment.

Henry for all his effrontery was not unmoved by the unrest among the populace, and the intransigence among the distinguished. He resolved to hew all the more closely to the line of schism without heresy, and in the latter part of his reign enacted the Six Articles popularly called "the bloody whip with the six strings" whereby a denial of the real presence was visited with death and clerical marriage was forbidden. Archbishop Cranmer, who had married the niece of one of the Continental reformers, was compelled during this period to keep his wife at home or when traveling to conceal her in a chest; when it was turned upside down she was somewhat inconvenienced — and ought to be included among the minor martyrs of the Reformation. The more ardent and advanced reformers were persecuted. Bishop Latimer spent the last years of Henry's reign in the Tower. Dr. Barnes and two others were sent to the stake. In the 1520's Barnes had aroused ire by appearing at least to condone the Anabaptist objection to law suits. He submitted and was treated as a reconciled heretic subject to house arrest. By feigning to commit suicide in the Thames he escaped to Wittenberg and there commenced his none too complimentary history of the popes. When Henry was desirous of currying Luther's support for the divorce, Barnes was commissioned as an agent, and in 1535 was brought back to England as a royal chaplain. Then, for his temerity in baiting the Bishop of Winchester, he was sent to the stake. This was the occasion when three Lutherans were burned and three friars beheaded, as a demonstration that Henry had taken the middle way. So things stood at the end of his reign. Schism without heresy — some disaffection but not enough to upset the regime.

Death intervened in 1547, and Henry was succeeded by the only son born to him by any of his six wives. Edward VI was only a lad of nine hailed by the reformers as a new Joshua. The title applied better to his maternal uncle, the Duke of Somerset, who assumed the regency with the title of Lord Protector. This is the time when England passed from schism to heresy, first to Lutheranism, then to Zwinglianism, and even Calvinism. No new English theology emerged, and even in this period of extreme Protestantism certain aspects of the policy of comprehension were apparent. The movement of the Reform, however, under Edward and Mary exhibited not so much combinations of diverse elements as zigzagging first to the left and then to the right, until a certain stabilization was achieved in the settlement of Elizabeth.

The reasons for the Protestant swing under Edward cannot be fixed with precision. The very release of pressure on the death of Henry no doubt had something to do with it. Cranmer was able to take his wife out of the chest and avail himself of his new liberty to adopt a more advanced view of the Lord's Supper. Latimer was released from the Tower and became court chaplain. He boldly informed His Highness from the pulpit that the function of the preacher is to correct kings as once he, Latimer, had rebuked Henry VIII for stabling horses in monasteries. Then

Latimer pitched into unpreaching prelates who, said he, are so "troubled with lordly living, rustling in their rents, dancing in their dominions, pampering their paunches, munching in their mangers, and loitering in their lordship, that they cannot attend to preaching." The English reformers were being reinforced by the influx of foreigners fleeing from the Roman Inquisition and the Augsburg Interim, men like Ochino at London, Vermigli at Oxford, Bucer at Cambridge, Laski the Pole at London, and John Knox in the north country. Among the natives there were punctilious precisionists like Hooper, the forerunner of Puritanism, who scrupled at the wearing of Aaronic vestments and desired to pull down the altars of Baal. All of these were for bringing Canterbury into line with Wittenberg, Zurich, and Geneva.

The Protector Somerset was not loath, but he was ineffectual because too tender for his times. He would have no constraint in religion and he essayed too much for one man, in that he sought at the same time to introduce genuine Protestantism, to cement Scotland and England in a plan of real equality, and to vindicate the farmers dispossessed through the enclosure of arable land for grazing in order to reap the profits of exporting wool to the looms of the Low Countries. He was frustrated by the mistrust of the Scotch, the greed of the proprietors, and a popular uprising, itself a curious blend of objection to the enclosures and to the Prayer Book in English. The Protector sympathized too much with the insurgents on the first count and was too loath to apply constraint on the second to take energetic measures. He was ousted by Northumberland, who dropped the Scots, worsted the rebels, and did not repudiate the Reform. On the contrary he allowed it to become more radical. The reign of Edward thus divides into two periods each of three years under the two protectors.

The protectorate of Somerset was marked by Lutheran leanings, that of Northumberland by Zwinglian and Calvinist tendencies. The changes are apparent not in doctrinal pronouncements; there was no official formulation of the doctrine of the Church of England until Elizabeth. Cranmer prepared forty-two articles which would have been promulgated had the king lived. As it is, the clue to doctrine is found in public worship. This is of itself indicative of the spirit of English comprehension which was not so much concerned to have everyone *think* alike as to *act* alike. Eternal salvation through correct belief was left to God and the individual, whereas the public aspects of religion were regulated by the state. All of this pointed toward latitudinarianism in belief and uniformity in practice.

The Book of Common Prayer appeared in two versions, the first in 1549 under Somerset, the second in 1552 under Northumberland. Both were the work of Cranmer in collaboration with numerous advisers. The first was basically Lutheran though at some points closer to the Mass, for whereas Luther expunged the canon because of the language of sacrifice, the Prayer Book was content to alter only specific expressions. At the same time the intent was to convert the Mass into the Holy Communion or Supper of the Lord. It should not be celebrated privately by the priest, but only in the presence of communicants. The wine as well as the bread should be given to the laity. The prayer was not that the bread and wine might *become*, but only that they might *be*, Christ's body and blood, thereby at least suggesting the repudiation of transubstantiation in favor of Luther's doctrine of concomitance. The spirit of comprehension is apparent in the retention of elements designed to conciliate the conservatives. Prayers were acknowledged not only for the living but also for the dead, and the formula of offering in communion was susceptible of a Lutheran and perhaps even of a Catholic interpretation: "The body of our Lord Jesus Christ which was given for thee preserve thy body and soul unto everlasting life."

The first Prayer Book was altogether unsatisfactory to the more radical Protestants. Whereas Calvin thought it full of "tolerable ineptitudes," Hooper considered it "manifestly defective, of dubious meaning and at some points plainly impious." Bucer made many specific suggestions for revision which Cranmer was the more ready to accept because he had for himself abandoned the doctrine of the real presence. For that reason everything even suggesting this view was eliminated or altered. The elements were given with the words: "Take and eat *this* [the word *this* was not further defined] in remembrance that Christ died for thee [which sounds Zwinglian] and feed on him in thy heart by faith with thanksgiving [which sounds Calvinist]. Drink this in remembrance that Christ's blood was shed for thee and be thankful [which again implies only the Zwinglian rite of commemoration]." The *Agnus Dei* ("Lamb of God"), sung by Catholics and Lutherans alike at the communion in token of the real presence, was expunged. The prayer of "humble access" before the communion, because interpreted as an act of adoration of the elements, was placed in advance of the consecration. Every reference to purgatory and prayers for the dead was removed. Gestures were forbidden, and among the vestments the use of the alb, chasuble, and cope. The priest became a minister, the altar a table, and the eucharist a commemoration.

Yet despite the move in a Protestant direction, this reign marked even more than that of Henry the perpetuation of the humanist ingredient in the English Reformation. This was the time when the works of Erasmus appeared in English dress, and notably by royal edict in 1547 his "Paraphrases on the Gospels" were to be placed in every church. The rendering into English was the joint endeavor of Protestants and Catholics. The work was sponsored by Katherine Parr, the widow of Henry VIII. One of the translators was Nicholas Udall, the father of English comedy. Another was the Princess Mary, who despite much bullying under Northumberland never abandoned the Mass. The Paraphrases represent that simple, undogmatic piety which is most conducive to the spirit of comprehension. The conclusion to the recital of the story of the prodigal son would not have satisfied Luther's demand for the exclusion of all merit and yet might if pressed be consonant with attributing all salvation to God. Erasmus wrote: "That the Father putteth the remembrance of himself in the son's mind is of his own beneficial goodness toward the son. But in that the son doth not neglect it when it is so put unto him, this is imputed to him as a thing meritorious, and the very confessing of the fault is received and accounted for satisfaction. He was lost through his own folly and was found again by his Father's love. And because he repented and emended even from the bottom of the heart for as much as he did truly mislike himself, his Father's mercifulness did not only restore him to his old dignity but made also a feast that he might commend and set forth his son to the hearty love of all that were belonging unto him."

Edward was followed by his half-sister Mary, a queen after all, and without the dire consequences over succession to prevent which Henry had made so many matrimonial ventures. Mary tried to undo the religious revolution inaugurated by her father and consummated by her brother, but in many respects she was unable to do so. The very return to Rome was achieved by royal initiative and parliamentary act; the determination of the form of religion was thus still a decision of the crown. She endeavored to restore to the church the confiscated wealth, but most of it was irrecoverably in private hands. Neither could the monasteries be revived half so readily as they had been dissolved. One thing she could do — elevate Catholics who had been in prison or exiled during the previous regimes. Cardinal Pole of royal lineage, whose mother Henry VIII had judicially murdered, was recalled from the Continent to restore Roman obedience. The Anglican bishops who for Romanist leanings had gone to the tower under Northumberland were given high posts, and on the other hand the leading reformers went into exile or to the stake. The foreigners were suffered to escape abroad: Vermigli, Ochino, Laski, Knox — Bucer was dead. The Edwardean bishops were sent to the fires of Smithfield. A contemporary records that 288 persons were burned during the reign of Mary, besides those that died of famine in sundry prisons.

Cranmer's execution was delayed because he had been consecrated by the pope and must await papal judgment. During the long interval he watched his colleagues, Ridley, Latimer, Hooper, and many another, go to the pyre. Shrinking from the stake was intensified by a genuine dilemma of conscience. He had always believed in and advocated the royal supremacy and now the royal supremacy returned the Church of England and the English nation to Roman

"THE FAYTHFUL APPREHENDED"

"The Picture or description of 22 godly and faythful Christians, apprehended about Colchester, pinioned together in one bande, and so with three leaders at the most, brought vp to London."

allegiance. If the crown could break with Rome, why could not the crown return to Rome? The difficulty of course was that submission to Rome meant relinquishment at any rate of the formula that the king was the supreme head of the church. But might not the principle be conserved without the formula — as in Spain or France where the crown managed without a breach to be supreme in the realm? Cranmer moved from a noncommittal submission to an abject recantation, but did not thereby save his life. He was called upon before execution to read his final abjuration, and to the amazement of all he concluded with these words: "And now I come to the great thing that so troubleth my conscience, and that is my sending abroad of writings contrary to the truth which here now I renounce and refuse as things written with my hand contrary to the truth which I thought in my heart, written for fear of death, and for as much as my hand offended in writing contrary to my heart, it shall be first burned." He was not suffered to finish but was dragged from the stage, and then with lively pace walked to the stake. As the flames leapt up he extended the offending hand until it was consumed.

Mary was followed by her half-sister, the Princess Elizabeth, daughter of Henry VIII and Anne Boleyn. Elizabeth was a Politique, concerned above all else for the security and tranquillity of the realm. As for her own position, she regarded the confessional differences as only a bagatelle. She agreed with the pope except upon some details, accepted the Augsburg Confession or something like it, and agreed with the Huguenots or very nearly. What would be politic under the circumstances was difficult to predict. If she were a Protestant she would be from the Catholic standpoint

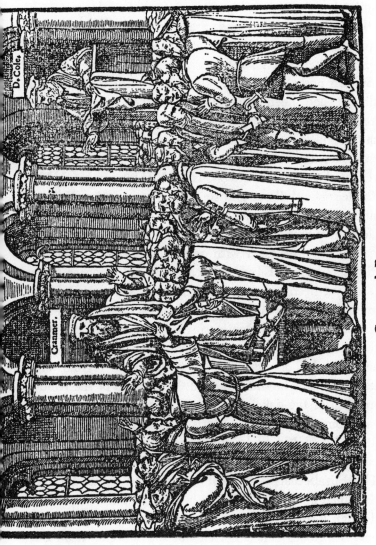

CRANMER'S RECOVERY

"The description of D. Cranmer, standing on the stage in S. Maries church, in the time of Coles Sermon, where he gaue the last confession of his faith, and was plucked downe therefore by the Fryers and other."

both a heretic and a bastard, and she might suffer from the combined opposition of Spain and France in league with Scotland. On the other hand, France and Spain were bound to quarrel, and to abet Protestants in the Netherlands might weaken both. At home the fires of Smithfield were a stench in English nostrils and Mary's marriage with the Spaniard Philip II had been unpopular. Whether courageous or meiely canny, Elizabeth decided for Protestantism coupled with the policy of comprehension with which she succeeded better than any other in that century. The reason was in part that she sought not like Charles V to comprehend alike Catholicism and Protestantism but only varieties of Protestantism. Charles moreover sought to impose the Interim by foreign troops, whereas Elizabeth embodied English nationalism. Charles dealt with people ineradicably rooted in Luther's teaching; Elizabeth headed a realm where there had not yet been a doctrinal formulation. Charles was confronted by a company of stout and trained opponents; Elizabeth inherited a situation in which successive purgings had extinguished extremists. There was in her reign, for example, a bishop who had survived every regime, and when asked how he did it replied, "I smacked of the willow more than of the oak." The oaks had gone down, many of them. Some indeed under Mary had escaped to the Continent and returned to be influential under Elizabeth; but even they were somewhat more willowy than the martyrs.

The Elizabethan settlement was marked by moderation and studied ambiguity. The oath required the renunciation of foreign jurisdiction but not specifically of the Bishop of Rome. Elizabeth called herself not the supreme head but only the supreme governor of the Church of England. The

Thirty-Nine Articles, the first doctrinal statement of the English church, were indeed definitely Protestant and not even the dextrous ingenuity of John Henry Newman in the nineteenth century could convert them into a document patient of Catholic interpretation. But they were not precise or altogether consistent with other promulgations of the reign. Particularly was this true with regard to the seat of authority. The twentieth article declares that "the Church hath power to decree rites or ceremonies." Elizabeth inserted "and authority in controversies of faith." But the article continues that the church is not to decree anything contrary to Holy Writ. But who is to determine what is contrary to Holy Writ is not explained. The next article asserts that general councils may err, whereas the Act of Suppression recognized the first four general councils. The spirit of comprehension is nowhere more manifest than in the new edition of the Book of Common Prayer, where the words of presentation from the two earlier versions were simply combined so that the minister says: "The body of our Lord Jesus Christ which was given for thee preserve thy body and soul unto everlasting life. Take and eat this in remembrance that Christ died for thee and feed on him in thy heart by faith and thanksgiving."

The studied ambiguities of the Elizabethan settlement can easily be exposed and readily scorned; but were they after all a less satisfactory solution of the strife of religions than the blinding clarity of the fires at Smithfield? And the Anglican Reformation is not in any case to be primarily appraised in the field of doctrine. Its greatest distinction was in worship. The Book of Common Prayer couches lofty supplications in superb prose, and more than all else has

11

The Struggle for Religious Liberty

THE FIGHT FOR RECOGNITION on the part of the confessions is a phase of the struggle for religious liberty, but only a limited phase. The confessions in the sixteenth century, apart from the Anabaptists, were not fighting for the right of each individual to worship as he pleased. The Catholic party roundly denounced toleration as the most culpable indifference, and Beza, the Calvinist, stigmatized religious liberty as "a most diabolical dogma because it means that every one should be left to go to hell in his own way." Each of the confessions was fighting only for its own right, and the possibility never so much as glimmered for most that divergent views might contain each a measure of truth, and that variance in practice even to the point of error might better be suffered than suppressed. The efforts of William of Orange proved abortive under the impact of Spanish fury and Calvinist iconoclasm, and the approximation momentarily achieved in Poland was due less to the doctrine of the inviolability of conscience, the integrity of personality, or the rights of man than to the anarchistic tendencies of feudalism which impeded any systematic interference. At the same time the age of the Reformation prepared the way in the realm of fact by breaking the monopoly of a single confession, and in the realm of idea elaborated all of the salient concepts which in the West came into their own through the Enlightenment.

These concepts are not specifically the offspring of the Reformation, though more readily operative in areas emancipated from papal sway. There were two main streams prior to the Reformation making for tolerance, and in confluence they were to be operative alike in Catholic and Protestant camps. One was mysticism, because to the mystic the concrete doctrines and forms of the Church are a matter of indifference. The union with God which is the goal of the mystic quest must be unconstrained and force is utterly ineffective either to produce or restrain it. The way to God is a way of trial and renunciation, which is more compatible with the sufferings of the martyr than with the torture chamber of the inquisitor.

The second great stream was the humanism of the Renaissance, because it espoused free inquiry and was sometimes tolerant of tentative gropings after truth even beyond the Christian fold. The free inquiry demanded by the movement as a whole, however, was very restricted and limited itself to the authenticity and correctness of historic Christian documents. This field should not be subject to dogmatic pronouncements by pope or councils who do not know of what they speak. The expert alone is qualified to have an opinion, and that opinion must be checked and corrected by the judgment of others equally competent. Truth is arrived at by a process of investigation, criticism and revision, and is never beyond re-examination. So long, however, as this point of view was confined to the study of documents, the humanist scholar might perfectly well persecute any defection from the articles of the faith. Among the Catholics the Cardinal Tournon was a humanist who would surely have burned Servetus had he not first fallen into the hands of Calvin, and among the Protestants, Melanchthon the humanist dragged Luther along the road which ended in the death penalty for even peaceable Anabaptists.

If, however, the method is extended from documents to dogmas, then the creedal formulations of the Church come to be regarded as tentative, and the historic statements of faith as only adumbrations of ultimate truth and as subject therefore to modification when fresh light should break from God's word. This whole attitude, which defines the faith less as a deposit than as a quest, makes for tolerance at least toward all the varieties of Christianity, and it may go even beyond. The universalism of the Renaissance was very kindly disposed to the pious heathen who lived before Christ and sometimes to those who by reason of locality had never heard of him. Even non-Christian religions might be regarded as preparations for the gospel, although no one in the sixteenth century went quite so far as Lessing in regarding the three rings of Christianity, Mohammedanism, and Judaism as indistinguishable. Such latitudinarianism was plainly a menace to the exclusive claims of Christianity, but for that very reason congenial to a world parliament of religions in which all should share and none should seek to dominate.

In the light of the preceding survey of the Protestant varieties, the deduction is obvious that religious liberty would flourish best among the Anabaptists who repudiated the union of church and state and among the Free Spirits so hospitable to mystical and rationalist tendencies. But religious liberty is not impossible and has in time actually been achieved on Lutheran, Calvinist, and likewise also on Catholic soil. The ideas which ministered to this outcome can be conveniently arranged by considering the nature of their attack upon the three walls which buttressed persecution. To persecute, a man must believe that he is right, that the point in question is important, and that coercion is effective.

On the first point the Catholics and the early reformers had not the least doubt. Christianity is the heir of the exclusive claims of Judaism. God is a jealous God who will suffer his people to have no gods before him. The prophets affirmed that no other gods existed. This God has a chosen people to whom he has bequeathed the land of promise. In Christianity to the one God was added the one Lord, and the land of promise became the life to come. For the early church the great struggle was not between the one God and the deities of polytheism, but between the one Lord and the Roman emperor. Christianity would suffer no rivals. She would die or conquer and she conquered. The certainties of the new faith rested upon the revelation of God in Christ as recorded in Scripture. The interpretation of Scripture came to be vested in the Church, and then free investigation was accorded only in peripheral areas on which as yet no definitive pronouncements had been made. But where the pope had spoken officially on faith and morals, no further discussion could be entertained, and those who in the Catholic Church of the sixteenth century called in question papal infallibility, which had not yet itself been infallibly declared, did so in the interests of conciliar authority and not of private judgment.

The Protestant Reformation swept away alike papal and conciliar authority, and when Luther asserted that on matters of faith and morals the pope could not determine but each must judge for himself, one would suppose that the principle of private judgment had been clearly enunciated. In a way it had, but certainly not in the sense subsequently current. Luther believed that if the Scripture were studied with the aid of all linguistic and critical tools its sense would become absolutely plain and no honest and competent inquirer would miss the meaning because the Holy Spirit would guide him to the true sense. If there were actually divergent interpretations, one would have to be wrong, and the Spirit lacking in the case of him who erred. Luther came to feel that the Holy Spirit was responsible not only for the Apostles' Creed and the Nicene Creed but even for the Augsburg Confession.

If the dissenter appealed to his conscience the reply was that conscience as such has no claims but only a *right* conscience. The word conscience is made up of two components, *con* and *scientia,* meaning "with knowledge." Only the correct conscience therefore is to be respected. This position of the early Protestants must appear as a retrogression over against the view already achieved by scholastic philosophers that conscience may be in error but is nevertheless binding until enlightened. This point the reformers might concede. To be sure, they would say, a man must not sin against his own lights and he is bound to do that which appears to him to be right even though he be mistaken; but he is entitled to no consideration for what he thinks to be right. What he thinks is neither here nor there. He must *be* right in order to have rights. In general this view was to prevail until well into the eighteenth century.

But even in the sixteenth, the citadels of certainty had been attacked. Erasmus was one of the first leaders of the onslaught. His contention was that Scripture is not clear. The text is uncertain and many passages are ambiguous and apparently contradictory. Critical acumen can do much to arrive at a correct text and the true meaning, but uncertainty remains and controversy itself is a proof of uncertainty because men do not wrangle over that which is perfectly obvious to all parties. If those who are equally equipped with the tools of scholarship are not of one mind, then the question cannot be plain. This line of approach was pursued with even greater radicalism by an Erasmian in the camp of Calvin. Sebastian Castellio was his name, a refugee from Savoy, a teacher for a time in the Genevan academy and later at Basel where he became a professor of Greek. The execution of Servetus filled him with profound indignation, and he set himself to examine and refute the grounds on which it was justified.

To this end he produced a book *On the Art of Doubting and of Knowing* in which he examined the principles of religious knowledge. His system was very largely empirical, reminding one of the Stoics before him and of John Locke afterwards. There are according to Castellio three sources of knowledge: experience, revelation, and reason. The first two are subject to the third, for clarification and elaboration. On this basis many of the traditional dogmas of the faith are incapable of conclusive demonstration and lie in the realm not of knowledge but of faith. The two must be clearly distinguished and what we believe we must not pretend to know.

All sects hold their religion according to the word of God and say that it is certain. Calvin says that his is certain and they affirm the same of theirs. He says that they are wrong and wishes to be the judge and so do they. Who shall be judge? Who made Calvin arbiter of all the sects that he alone should kill? He has the word of God, but so have they. If the matter is so certain to whom is it certain? To Calvin? There is nothing unknown to him. He talks as if he might be in Paradise. But why then does he write so many books about manifest truth, and such huge tomes to explain what he says is absolutely clear?

This line of approach led to a distinction between those teachings which because controverted are uncertain, including the Trinity, the Lord's Supper, baptism, predestination and the state of souls after death; and on the other hand, those teachings which, because unchallenged, may be assumed to be true, such as the existence of God, the creation of the world, immortality and the moral law, all of them scarcely questioned in that age. In the area of common consent constraint would be admissible if this argument alone were adduced.

The difference between Catholicism and Protestantism in the use of this approach was less marked in the early years of the century than it was subsequently to become. To the Erasmians it was congenial, but Erasmianism was to succumb to Tridentine Catholicism. Protestantism on the other hand in its dominant branches became at first more dogmatic in the seventeenth century but in the eighteenth went so far beyond Erasmus that the Deistic movement reduced Christianity to little more than that which it had in common with Confucianism. The demolition of ecclesiastical dogmatism proved, however, of itself to be no guarantee of liberty, for in the French Revolution reason and skepticism sent their victims to the guillotine.

The second prerequisite for persecution was more significant: that the point in question should be considered important. To be willing to put dissenters to death a group must be convinced that its security is imperiled at some vital spot. Even waves of hysteria conjure up a supposed peril to inflame and justify passions. The greatest persecutors in the history of Christianity have not been hypocrites or monsters, but the devotees of an ideal which they believed to be of supreme importance for mankind. In their judgment man's eternal destiny as well as his social well-being are contingent upon the good pleasure of God vouchsafed only to those who believe correctly, worship rightly, and belong to the Church which He has ordained as an ark of Noah outside of which no souls are saved. In this picture orthodox belief was considered of greater importance than upright conduct, because the man who accepts the teachings may mend his life, whereas he who rejects them, though irreproachable at the moment, is almost bound to disintegrate because the faith is the only sound ground for morals. Since the Church is the shrine of all well-being she should seek to permeate all institutions with her spirit, whether the school or the state, and the arm of the latter should be at her disposal for the suppression of dissent, because fear of the stake may recall a heretic from his error or at least restrain him from open profession and the corruption of others. If he persists, his removal is like the amputation of a limb to save a life.

Such was the theory. The advocates of liberty tore it apart and leveled their attack upon it piece by piece. First came the assumption that right belief is necessary in order to insure eternal blessedness. The reply was that the picture of a God consigning men to eternal torment because of error is a monstrous perversion of the Christian view of God the Father. Erasmus wrote a tract entitled *On the Immense Mercy of God.*

They are not impious [he wrote] who utterly deny the existence of God as are those who portray Him as inexorable. Throughout the Gospels the whole house rings with exultation because the son that was dead is alive. A shepherd brings home the lost sheep upon his shoulders, and the father places the robe upon the prodigal and the ring upon his finger and kills for him the fatted calf. Christ wept over Jerusalem because he *could* not save this poor people and we talk as if he *would* not.

A disciple of Erasmus among the Protestants, an Italian refugee at Basel named Curio, composed a book on *The Wideness of God's Kingdom* in which he envisaged the salvation of all peoples. Obviously he was rejecting the doctrine of reprobation which was a corollary of predestination. For this view he would substitute universalism, entailing the eventual and indeed the speedy conversion of all peoples to the faith. At that moment England had embraced the Reformation and Poland appeared to be on the verge. An expectation of a change among the Turks and the Jews was not too sanguine a hope for one who expected God to employ an angel for the conversion of the Americas. One who had such confidence in missionaries and angels had no need for magistrates to advance the faith.

And if God were ready to damn for all eternity he would not do so over a matter of dogma so much as over a question of behavior. For the liberals, deeds were to be esteemed as more important in God's eyes than creeds. Erasmus constantly based his pleas for Luther on the ground that he was irreproachable in his life. And Castellio exclaimed:

This man you say is a heretic, a putrid member to be cut off from the body of the Church lest he infect others. But what has he done? Oh, horrible things. Yes, but what? Is he a murderer, an adulterer, a thief? No. What then? Does he not believe in Christ and the Scriptures? Certainly he does, and would rather die than not continue in his belief. But he does not understand them correctly, that is, he interprets them differently from our teachers. This is a capital offense to be expiated in the flames.

The whole ethical approach regarded good deeds as the test of creeds, and adjudged that faith to be the better which makes the better man. Good deeds were even considered to be the condition of right creeds, since only the pure in heart can see God. The Scriptures can be understood only by those who love and obey Christ. This was a point very dear to the Anabaptists and to obey Christ meant for them to imitate his meekness and his mercy.

The emphasis among those committed to the rational and ethical approach was upon sincerity rather than upon inerrancy as the condition for God's favor. Sincerity is an interior loyalty to that which at the moment appears to be true. Castellio went so far as to say that to tell the truth is to say what one believes to be true. On this basis he could declare that Servetus had been put to death for telling the truth inasmuch as by lying and denying his convictions he could have been saved. He perished because he would not recant. The reason why sincerity is so prized is because integrity is indispensable in the quest for truth. There is no deposit of dogma equally valid whether professed by the sincere or the insincere. Rather there is a truth which can be seized only by those who pursue it with passion and utter transparency.

The view that membership in the visible Church is necessary for salvation was naturally undercut by the mystics, for whom the true fellowship can never be captured and confined within the frame of an institution. Again the Latitudinarians of the Renaissance, who looked upon all religions as so many spokes leading into the same hub, could not attach salvation exclusively to any one, and the Universalists who dreamed of the ultimate salvation of all men plainly did not regard membership in any single organization as indispensable.

A halfway position was taken by those who made a distinction between dogmas some of which are essential and some not. The concept of Fundamentalism arose in this connection. At that time it was the attempt to reduce the fundamentals to the smallest number in order that constraint might be restricted to this minimal area and all else left free. The distinction of course was an old one. The Church had always differentiated the cardinal tenets from the minor. The anti-dogmatic groups of the late Middle Ages had gone further and pointed out how little dogma is necessary for salvation and that of course was the whole point, not how much is true but how much needs to be known and believed in order to be saved. The penitent thief was the classic example of one who was admitted by Christ to Paradise without any preparatory instruction. All he believed was that there is a Paradise and that Christ had the authority to admit him.

This idea was worked out in much greater detail by another Italian Protestant refugee, Acontius by name. For a time he was at Basel, and later was employed by Queen Elizabeth in London as an engineer on the Thames embankment. He wrote a book entitled *On the Wiles of Satan* in which he converted the medieval argument that the devil was busy destroying souls by stirring up heresy into the argument that Satan was doing his deadly work by inciting persecution. We must be extremely careful, argued Acontius, not to force men over points which God has not declared to be necessary. None of the points controverted among Protestants such as predestination, the Lord's Supper, and baptism were on his list of essentials. Scripture, he claimed, stipulates only two necessary beliefs. The first is that the just are saved by faith. This principle excludes the Catholics who rely on good works. The second is, "Believe on the Lord Jesus Christ and thou shalt be saved." This verse would exclude those who deny the Lord Jesus, though what constituted denial was not defined by Acontius. His ideas became very influential and in an English translation may well have guided the policy of Cromwell, who excluded from his settlement the Roman Catholics and the Unitarians. But it was a dangerous argument, capable of being reversed. Some contended that if an error on the nonessentials does not entail damnation, then the regulation of belief on all such points should be committed to the government, and freedom allowed only in the area of the essentials which had previously been reduced to such minimal terms. This inference was used in defense of the Augsburg Interim and also of the Anglican settlement.

Many extraneous considerations of course also entered to minimize the importance of the points on which constraint was exercised in the age of the Reformation. Nationalism diverted interest from orthodoxy to patriotism. The mercantile age subordinated confessional niceties to the exigencies of the ledger. Growing secularism tended to make an anachronism of one who would either die or kill for a religious belief. Only the rise in modern times of a new secularism with a faith so intense that for it men will die, kill and lie, and the coincident discovery that the only force capable of persistent resistance is the Christian faith, have brought back the mood of the martyr to whom the persecutor is not altogether unintelligible.

Once again this second line of approach is more con-

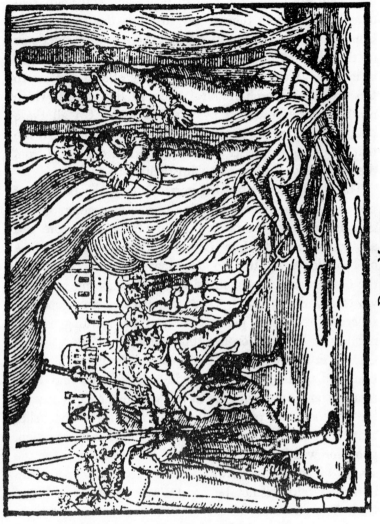

DUTCH MARTYRS

genial to Protestantism than to Catholicism, which cannot dissociate salvation from correct belief and still holds that outside the Church there is no salvation, though the term Church is so broadly construed that those beyond the doors of the visible Church are not necessarily lost. The shift in emphasis from the theological to the ethical appears to the Catholic Church inimical even to the ethical which must itself be sustained by a sound faith. On all these points Protestantism is more flexible, though not unaware that an undue emphasis on the ethical is a departure from the centrality of religion in Christianity.

The third prerequisite for persecution is the belief that coercion can be effective. None of the persecutors of the sixteenth century entertained any doubt on that score and an inquisitor in the Low Countries remarked at the time of Tyndale's trial, "It is no great matter, whether they that die on account of religion be guilty or innocent, provided we terrify the people by such examples; which generally succeeds best when persons eminent for learning, riches, nobility or high station are thus sacrificed." The Catholic Church in the twentieth century no longer takes this position, and on the score of expediency Catholics and Protestants stand on equal ground in their readiness to forsake the methods once practiced by their forebears. The belief that persecution is good for something provokes the question, good for what? If it be held that it is of efficacy for the saving of souls the answer is that salvation depends on faith and faith cannot be constrained. Faith is a gift of God. This statement of the Apostle Paul became a slogan for the advocates of liberty in all confessions and in all lands. If faith is a gift of God, then it can no more be created by the sword of the magistrate than a wall can be

constructed by blasting with cannon balls. No one said
this earlier or better than Luther in the age of the Reformation. "Faith," he said, "is a free work to which no
one can be forced It is a divine work in the spirit. Let
alone then that outward force should compel or create it."
For that reason Luther long held out against any penalty
more severe than banishment and even to the end endeavored to conserve his formula that faith is not to be
coerced, but only blasphemy and sedition rather than heresy
are to be penalized because they attack the public order
of church, state and society.

The liberals commonly argued that the doctrine of predestination should preclude persecution, since if salvation
is predetermined no amount of force can alter the situation.
Usually for themselves they rejected the doctrine of predestination as to salvation while substituting for it an
intellectual determinism on the ground that the mind cannot
assent to that to which it does not assent, any more than
the eye can see as red that which it sees as blue. Constraint
will not mend matters. In some cases this determinism
is absolute. A moron can never grasp an argument. But
in other cases the difficulty is that apperception is slow and
impeded by many obstacles. In order to effect conversion
we must then master the art of persuasion. To this strategy
Acontius devoted one of the most significant sections of his
book *On the Wiles of Satan*. "The greatest hindrances to
clear sight," said he, "are passion, pride and prejudice, and
these are only accentuated by vainglory and arrogance on
the part of the one who is seeking to persuade. Humility
and manifest devotion to truth are the prime requisites
for winning converts." Beneath this method of Acontius
is of course the assumption that truth in the long run will

command assent. The discovery that truth does not so swiftly take care of herself was what led Luther to deflect from his earlier liberal course.

If the contention is that persecution is good for the Church, the reply is that the number may be increased but the quality will not be improved. Persecution if it does not make martyrs contrives to turn heretics into hypocrites. Castellio observed, "I say that those who have regard to numbers and on that account constrain men, gain nothing but rather lose and resemble a fool, who having a great barrel with a little wine in it, fills it up with water to get more. But instead of increasing the wine he spoils what he had. . . . The gospel was forced on England under Edward VI but the accession of Mary revealed how few were genuinely persuaded. The Jews in Spain, who have been baptized by force, are no more Christian than before."

If the claim be that persecution is good for the state, the answer is that on the contrary it may serve to provoke sedition. The Anabaptists were eventually goaded into revolution after being subjected to ten years of extermination, and the Huguenots after thirty years of offering themselves as lambs for the slaughter at last struck back. Such facts were not lost on that generation, and Castellio observed that "tyranny engenders sedition which arises from the attempt to force and kill heretics rather than to let them live without constraint." When the Catholic opponents of Luther urged the enforcement of the Edict of Worms on the ground that his teaching was subversive to the civil state, the reply was that the attempt to apply the Edict would itself provoke rebellion.

Deeper than all the arguments bandied back and forth by a goodly company of advocates was a deeply rooted conviction of the incompatibility between the cross and the stake. Suffering is the lot and the mark of the Christian. He must be as the sheep and not as the wolf. If he is to follow his Master he must ascend Calvary and not the judgment hall of Pilate or of Herod.

Which among all the factors making for religious liberty have been the most potent obviously cannot be determined. Prudential considerations have played their part. Yet one cannot feel that the witness of the martyrs and the pleas for mercy have gone unheeded.

12

The Reformation and the
Political Sphere

To ASSESS THE EFFECTS of the Reformation on the social life
of Europe is no simple matter. To begin with there is a
dispute whether religion can be regarded as a determinative
force in human affairs or whether religious slogans are merely
a screen for mundane motives. The economic and sociological determinists will explain for example the religious communism of the Hussites or the Anabaptists as due not to
a reading of the Book of Acts but as in some way connected
with the development of silver mines in Bohemia. Just
how this will explain the strength of Anabaptists in the
Netherlands is difficult to see. Some explain the Protestant
movement itself as a rebellion of the Teutonic peoples against
the dominance of the Latins. This generalization is not
devoid of truth because obviously in the end Protestantism
became established in the north and Catholicism in the
south. The great exception of course was Ireland where
Catholicism became the rallying point of the struggle against
England. Yet this approach must not be overdone since
the demarcation between the confessions would never have
been so sharp had it not been for the principle of territorialism and the expulsion of minorities. Had there been

THE REFORMATION AND THE POLITICAL SPHERE

no exchange of populations Protestantism would have been much more extensive in the south, especially in France, and by the same token Catholicism would have retained a greater hold in the north.

Again the revolt against Rome is accounted for on the score of resentment against economic exploitation, and this factor as one among others cannot be gainsaid. On the other hand particular grievances could have been adjusted by national concordats with Rome, such as the one conceded to France, and without any repudiation of the spiritual jurisdiction of the papacy. Finally some historians interpret the Reformation in terms of social classes. Catholicism is said to have been the religion of the upper classes, Lutheranism and Calvinism of the middle, and Anabaptism of the lower. Such an explanation overlooks the fact that the sixteenth century was devoid of that sharp social stratification which came later as a development from the industrial revolution. Furthermore the complexion of the religious groups has been misread. The Anabaptists were not Anabaptists because they were disinherited. They were disinherited because they were Anabaptists. The early leaders came from the burgher intelligentsia. Lutheranism is supposed to have lost all agrarian constituency after the Peasants' War, but as a matter of fact Luther's congregation at Wittenberg never ceased to be composed largely of peasants. In the succeeding centuries in certain lands the enterprising merchants were Calvinists, but were they Calvinist because enterprising or enterprising because Calvinist?

Those who explain religion in economic and sociological fashion are not readily disposed to reverse the roles and recognize that religion itself has altered the economic and social pattern. The uniqueness of one school of historians is that they do give a religious interpretation to social change. Some of them would range Protestantism and notably Calvinism among the forces making for the rise of the spirit of capitalism. In the political area Catholicism is reckoned as the prototype for absolutism, Lutheranism is held responsible for the development in Germany of totalitarianism, and Calvinism is credited with the rise of democracy in England and New England. In the domestic field the abolition by Protestantism of monasticism is held to have exalted the home as the sphere for the exercise of the gentler Christian virtues.

The point of view of this book is one which recognizes a continuous and intricate interplay, so intricate indeed that the factors are often very difficult to isolate. Take first the area of political thought and action. The great change in progress in the political structure of Europe was the rise of nationalism. It was prompted by the craving for security. The Holy Roman Empire never succeeded in suppressing feudal warfare, and what had not been achieved on the larger scale was then undertaken on a smaller regional basis within the confines of the new nations. The Roman Church both abetted and resisted the process. Assistance was given to the national states in order to weaken the Empire, but obstruction was practiced wherever they sought to bring ecclesiastical revenues and appointments under local control. In the meantime Protestantism threw its weight behind the national states wherever they were engaged in conflict with Rome, but not out of any predilection for nationalism as such. The Lutheran princes in Germany cherished rather the Empire and in the Thirty Years' War often suffered their scruples against its dismemberment to impede the most strategic course in the defense of their faith. The main concern of Protestants at all times was not for any particular form of the state but for liberty to practice what they conceived to be the true religion. On the eastern border, as previously noted, the rule of the Turk was preferred by the Protestants to that of the Hapsburgs because the Turk was religiously neutral but the Hapsburg fanatically Catholic. If the story be reviewed one observes that Protestantism was allied with the struggle for national independence in Sweden and Holland but Catholicism played this role in Ireland. In France and Poland Protestantism attached itself to the feudal nobility against the crown, but if the crown became favorable, then Protestants veered to loyalism. In Germany Protestantism was espoused by the free cities and the territorial princes in a system lying somewhere between feudalism and nationalism.

On the great political problems of the age the lines do not coincide neatly with the religious confessions. The consuming problem of the sixteenth century was whether the state is to be regarded as a moral organism or simply as a power bloc. The great exponents of the ethical state were Erasmus and Thomas More, and of the amoral state Machiavelli. Formally at least they were all Catholic. The difference between them is discovered by some historians in their divergent situations. The moralists are said to have been those whose countries were not subject to intense pressures and whose security depended upon peace among their neighbors. More was an Englishman, the citizen of an island, enjoying the relative security afforded by the Channel. Erasmus was a Hollander, the son of a little state devoid completely of security unless the great powers kept the peace or at least respected her neutrality. For these reasons More and Erasmus are said to have counseled Christian restraint, conciliation, and the application of reason to politics. But Machiavelli was a Florentine, the secretary of a city-state depending for its existence upon a precarious balance of power to be maintained by eternal vigilance and a callous disregard in extremities for scruples of conscience. Erasmus entertained an optimism as to the possibility of conserving and enhancing the unities of Europe and was forever inveighing against the folly and crime of war between fellow Christians. His prescription was a combination of Christian tolerance and political isolationism. Let each state renounce imperialism and concentrate on good government within its present domains. Machiavelli, on the other hand, despaired of anything beyond oases of security to be established and maintained only by tolerating no nonsense within or without.

If one compares Protestant political thinking with these ideas often Luther is associated with Machiavelli and the Anabaptists with Erasmus. The Calvinists do not quite fit this pattern. But even the first two associations are only most superficially correct. Luther was emphatically not Machiavellian. The Saxon reformer could never regard the security of a particular state as the chief end of man. He would rather have seen the land infested by an army of occupation than that it should defend itself in a manner contrary to the command of Christ. Luther unquestionably called for the use of the sword without reservation in order to suppress rebellion on the part of those not authorized by Scripture to take the sword. But treachery or any violation of the traditional code of the just war was to him utterly abhorrent. He was on the side of Erasmus in regarding the state as a moral organism, though very much less optimistic than Erasmus as to the possibility of a European peace or of regulating human affairs around a conference table. He was closer to Machiavelli's pessimism regarding human behavior and looked to force more than to persuasion to hold the recalcitrant in check.

As for the Anabaptists, their pacifism was much more drastic than that of Erasmus and much less optimistic. Curiously their estimate of human nature did not markedly diverge from that of Machiavelli and Luther, but the moral for them was that the saints should dissociate themselves from the corrupt world and seek in some remote spot to establish the ideal commonwealth. The Calvinist pattern does not exactly fit anywhere because it was a combination of optimism and pessimism, inasmuch as men were held to be quite depraved, yet God through groups of the chosen could erect not simply a segregated community of saints but a Holy Commonwealth in the midst of an evil world. To this end force was held to be indispensable but should never be exercised without regard to moral restraints.

When a comparison is made between the political consequences of Lutheranism and Calvinism the common generalization is that Lutheranism made for totalitarianism and Calvinism for democracy. There can be no question that in Germany, and notably in Prussia, Lutheranism became a state church. The Bismarckian policy had the support of the Lutherans, whereas Catholics in Germany, and only in Germany in the nineteenth century, were allied with political liberalism. A further step is taken by some interpreters who say that Lutheranism paved the way for National Socialism by teaching implicit obedience to the commands of the state. On the other hand, Calvinism in France, England, Scotland, and New England was associated with revolution and even tyrannicide. The indisputable

LUTHER, THE ELECTOR JOHN FREDERICK, AND MELANCHTHON

facts in this picture are that Lutheranism was the established church in Germany at the time of the rise of National Socialism and that Calvinism in various lands has been the party of revolution. At the same time one must not forget that the state church in Germany in the twentieth century was a combination of the Lutheran and the Reformed, nor can one overlook the fact that the Confessional Church, which opposed Hitler, was also Lutheran and that in the Scandinavian lands Lutheranism has not issued in totalitarianism. On the score of Calvinism one must bear in mind that in France, whenever the monarchy was favorable to the Huguenots, Calvinist political thinking veered to royalism. All of this suggests that in these instances circumstance had more effect than religion upon the political theories of religious bodies. Rather one might say that for all Protestants religion transcended politics and the chief concern was to give free course to the Word of God. Just as the Catholic Church will make a concordat with any regime which allows freedom to administer the sacraments, freedom to propagate the faith, freedom to hold property, and freedom for the monastic orders, so Protestantism has been willing to tolerate any form of government which accords religious liberty to Protestantism.

Certain differences in emphasis, however, can be discerned between the Protestant groups and they center again largely on diversity of circumstance. Luther indubitably stressed the duty of obedience to government. He did so precisely because he was being taxed with disobedience. His papal opponents did their best to besmirch him with the charge of political subversiveness, and the Edict of Worms pronounced him to be more dangerous to the civil than to the ecclesiastical power. Against all such accusations he replied with a stormy denial, but to assume that he meant thereby to inculcate unqualified submission to government would be utterly to misconstrue his meaning. There were two instances in which he recognized the duty of civil disobedience. The first was in case the government commanded anything contrary to the faith. The second was if the government embarked upon an unjust war. In accord with Catholic teaching Luther held that ordinarily the government itself would be the judge of the justice of the war. Nevertheless if the citizen were in a position to know that the war was not just, he should then refuse to serve. Positive armed resistance to government was another matter. Luther at first opposed it altogether. The gospel should never be defended by the sword. Public order might be defended by the sword, but rebels and especially those using religious slogans should be suppressed alike for the crime of rebellion and for the sacrilege of bloodshed on behalf of the gospel. The magistrate was in a different category and, as earlier noted, Luther was gradually brought by the jurists to the conclusion that even the highest magistrate, the emperor himself, was not absolute but only a constitutional monarch who, if he violated the constitution, could be brought to book, resisted, and deposed by the princes of the realm. This was the doctrine of the right of the lower magistrate to protect the people against the tyranny of the higher. So commonly is this idea associated with Calvinism that one is prone to overlook its origin on Lutheran soil. The first great statement of the principle occurred in the Magdeburg Confession of 1550. But after the Peace of Augsburg in 1555, when Lutheranism gained legal recognition, the need for invoking this theory was gone in Germany. Its supporters came rather to be found in the Calvinist ranks.

The locality where political absolutism in the sixteenth century received the greatest support from churchmen was England, and since England in the twentieth century has been the bulwark of democracy one must beware of attributing too much influence to the force of sixteenth-century ideas. England under the Tudors reached the high peak of monarchical power. Henry VIII exercised an arbitrariness of control the like of which was known neither under his predecessors nor his successors. The term used to describe the Tudor view of the relations of church and state is Erastianism, a word derived from the name of an obscure Swiss theologian, Erastus. It is the view that the form of religion may be determined by the civil power. Some such theory was necessary to justify the principle of territorialism even when infused with the spirit of comprehension. This position is frequently taken to mean, as it did to Thomas More, that the state has an absolute control over religion. The point was brought out in the examination of More by Mr. Riche, the king's solicitor who said:

"Admitt there were, Sir, an Acte of Parliament, that all the Realme should take me for King, would you not take me for King?"

"Yes sir," quoth Sir Thomas More, "that I would."

"I put the case further," quoth Mr. Riche, "that there weare an Acte of Parliament that all the Realme should take me for the Pope; would then not you, Mr. More, take me for the Pope?"

"To your first case," quoth Sir Thomas More, "the Parliament may well meddle with the stat of temporall Princes; but to make aunsweare to your second case, I will put you this case: suppose the Parliament would make a law that God should not be God, would you then, Mr. Riche, saye God weare not God?"

More was unquestionably right that matters of religious belief cannot be determined by an Act of Parliament, but Erastianism in practice never claimed so much. The existence of a Christian community was always assumed and the point was to know where jurisdiction lay in the settlement of its external forms and its practical administration. The Middle Ages had long debated the relative roles of the pope and the emperor as the heads of Christendom. Papalism vied with Caesaropapism. The ideal of the Middle Ages was parallelism, though on occasion the emperors did not hesitate to summon councils and to make and unmake popes. The canon lawyers countered by claiming for the pope jurisdiction over the two keys, spiritual and secular—that is, over church and state. No imperialists in that age retorted by reversing the assertion and ascribing the two keys to the emperor. This culmination of the claims of the state came to pass only after the rise of nationalism, when adduced on behalf of the Tudor monarchy by Archbishop Cranmer who, changing somewhat the figure, asserted that both the sword and the keys are wielded by the king.

But certainly Cranmer never contemplated the possibility of the establishment of atheism. Nor at the time did he envisage a return to the authority of Rome; and when Mary Tudor took just that course, he found himself in a frightful dilemma of conscience not remote from that of Thomas More. The Catholic testified to his faith at the block, the Protestant expiated his concession to the civil power at the stake. The Church at no time was willing for long to acquiesce in a regime of political absolutism in the field of religion. Yet the fact remains that the first approach to such totalitarianism occurred in England when Henry made himself the "supreme head of the Church," and the doctrine of Erastianism could suggest that the very existence of God depended on an Act of Parliament. Until the Calvinist invasion England was the land where Protestantism was most compliant toward the national state. Only during the Puritan Revolution did England become the seed plot of democracy.

For the second half of the sixteenth century Calvinism was the party of revolution and the scene was France. Circumstance more than the initial presuppositions of Luther and Calvin contributed to this outcome. The only essential difference between the founders lay in Calvin's greater hopefulness for the erection of a divine society through God's chosen instruments. The use of force was not a necessary corollary and Calvin himself was most reluctant to countenance carnal weapons. But the spirit of enterprise which the ideal engendered might and did become less chary as to the means.

The arguments used by the Calvinists to legitimatize the right of revolution may seem very farfetched and one may wonder why they bothered with arguments at all. The reason was that they were quite as much appalled as their opponents by the prospect of anarchy and wished to make plain that their revolution moved within very circumscribed limits. At first they pretended not to be fighting the King of France, but rather to be seeking his deliverance from his evil entourage, the Guises. It was the same defense employed at first by the English Puritans when they claimed not to be fighting Charles I but only the Malignants by whom he was surrounded and seduced. The fiction was rendered utterly untenable in France when the king himself, Charles IX, instigated the Massacre of St. Bartholomew. Thereafter Huguenot thought became frankly revolutionary.

But there was still a question as to the persons who might properly wield the sword. The feeling was very deep rooted that to commit the sword to that many-headed monster, the common man, was bound to issue in chaos. Hence the earnest attempt to keep the revolt within the channels of legitimacy and the restriction by Calvin of the right of revolution only to the princes of the blood, namely the Bourbons. When they proved to be broken reeds, more radical ideas were advanced. A tentative proposal was that the king, if he violated the laws of nature or the constitution of the realm, ceased thereby at once to be king and might be resisted by anyone without fear of impiety.

In this contention there was already implicit a theory of the origin and character of kingly power as bounded by law written or unwritten. The next step was to make royal prerogative derivative from popular sovereignty. The eventual form of the doctrine was the contract theory of government. But the contract theory was secular and the Calvinist view was thoroughly religious. The word *contract* is not so appropriate to describe the position as the word *covenant*. The proof text was found in the Second Book of Kings in the eleventh chapter, seventeenth verse. "And

Jehoiada made a covenant between the Lord and the king and the people that they should be the Lord's people; between the king also and the people."

The theory was well explained in a tract by one of the French Huguenots, *The Vindication against Tyrants* (1579):

The covenant is double between God and the king and between God and the people. Each is bound to see that the Church be not damnified. If Israel forsake God and the king makes no account of it, he is justly guilty of Israel's delinquency. In like manner if the king follow after strange gods and Israel seek not to withdraw him from his rebellion, they make the fault of their king their own transgression. But who may punish the king if it be not the whole body of the people to whom the king swears and obliges himself no more and no less than do the people to the king. We read also that King Josias, together with the whole people, made a covenant with the Lord, the king, and the people promising to keep the laws and ordinances of God.

The author of this tract was still very fearful lest his doctrine give the handle to ultra-democratic conclusions and therefore sought still to revert to the older theory of revolution vested only in the lower magistrates. "What shall be answered," he inquires, "to the objection that a whole people, that beast of many heads, must run in mutinous disorder?" To which he answers that by the people he means "those who hold their authority from the people, that is the magistrates who are inferior to the king."

Prolonged provocation increasingly broke down lingering reservations. When Bloody Mary in England was sending the Protestant bishops to the fires of Smithfield, those already steeped in the doctrines of Geneva, and earlier than in France, voiced a less qualified right of resistance. Christopher Goodman in his tract *How Superior Powers Ought to be Obeyed* (1558) averred:

This zele to defend Gods Lawes and preceptes, wherewith all sortes of men are charged, it is not onely prayseworthie in all, but requyred of all to see the judgmentes thereof executed vpon all manner of persones without exception. And that if it be not done by the consent and ayed of the Superiours, it is lawfull for the people, yea it is their duetie to do it themselves, as well vpon their owne rulers and Magistrat, as vpon other of their brethren, to cut of euery rotten membre. If death be deserued, death.

Likewise Bishop Ponet, writing in 1556, affirmed the lawfulness of killing a tyrant to be "graffed in the hearts of men. This lawe testifieth to euery mannes conscience, that it is naturall to cutte awaie an incurable membre, Kinges, Princes and other gouernours, albeite they are the headdes of the politike body, yet they are not the hole body. And though they be the chief membres, yet they are but membres; nother are the people ordained for them, but they are ordained for the people."

John Knox left no doubt as to what this doctrine meant in his interview with Mary, who inquired whether he thought subjects having power might resist their princes. "If their princes exceed their bounds, Madam, it is no doubt that they may be resisted even by power." When Mary protested that the Apostles had not so resisted their persecutors, Knox replied that the reason was solely the lack of funds.

Plainly such views cut athwart political absolutism and end in the doctrine of the limited sovereignty of the state, even though they fall far short of democratic equalitarianism. But whether Protestantism, and particularly Calvinism, should be given exclusive credit at this point can only be denied, when it is observed that the political thinking of the Catholics, when out of power, moved in precisely the same direction. The Jesuits were the heirs of the Calvinists in espousing the doctrine of revolution against an heretical monarch.

The claim that all of the religious contestants of the sixteenth century contributed to modern democracy at the point of denying state absolutism is incontestable. For all of these bodies the state was limited by a demarcation of sphere. Some held indeed that church and state might appropriately be united and that the state might aid the true religion and suppress the false. But all insisted that the state might not constrain the true religion and each believed its own to be the true. Others like the Anabaptists called for a separation of church and state and a very sharp separation of spheres. Again all of the religious bodies combatted absolutism because of their belief in a universal morality, the law of nature, binding upon all states whether Christian or non-Christian. The Machiavellian claim that the state may be a law unto itself could never have been tolerated by any Christian body.

If democracy be defined in terms of popular participation in government the contribution is less obvious. Lutheranism grew up amid and found congenial a feudal patriarchalism within political units scarcely larger than squirarchies in which the needs of the common man could be ascertained and met by consultation rather than by ballots. Calvinism espoused equalitarianism and full participation in the common life only for the saints. The system made for an aristocracy of the elect. The Anabaptist pattern held the greatest ultimate promise for a transfer of Congregationalism from the meetinghouse to the town hall because of the separation of church and state. So long as the two are united the saints hesitate to admit the strangers to equal privileges lest the church become subject to alien control. Only after that fear is eliminated through separation will churchmen readily consent to an exercise of the franchise by all the inhabitants of the community. In the sixteenth century the ideas of the Anabaptists, so long as they were exiled to the frontiers, could not come to fruition. For the full outworking one needs to turn to their spiritual successors, the Baptists, the Independents, and the Quakers in the seventeenth century alike in England and the New World.

13

The Reformation and the
Economic and Domestic Spheres

IN THE FIELD OF ECONOMICS a phenomenon comparable in the sixteenth century to the rise of nationalism was the emergence of capitalism. The term *capitalism* is used in varying senses. It signifies something more than commerce on however imposing a scale. Capitalism has reference to a system of production and distribution. One of its marks is individualism. The corporate guild structure of the Middle Ages gave way to a system in which the entrepreneur for himself produced and sold in unrestrained competition. The workers likewise were individually hired and fired. The guild system became the factory. The system expanded by disposing of products beyond local need in distant parts. For such an enterprise money, credit, bookkeeping, and banking were required. Business was systematized. The whole process was stimulated by the ambition of Renaissance man to bring all areas of life under rational control. Here lies the difference between the capitalist and the merchant adventurer or the great moneylender, both essentially medieval types, because they did not reduce their endeavors to system. The distinction, however, in actual life was not sharp and the Fuggers, for example, exhibited mixed characteristics. They made their initial fortune in textiles in a system anticipatory of the new captalism, but they used their wealth for moneylending. By defaulted securities they acquired vast holdings in mines which enabled them to lend on so gigantic a scale as to be able to finance alike the papacy and the Holy Roman Empire. At this point, however, they were still glorified pawnbrokers rather than capitalists in the proper sense.

Again the term *capitalism* has been used to describe not so much a system as a spirit, an attitude toward life, a fury of work in gainful employ. This phenomenon is peculiar to the Western world. In the East men work in order to attain a certain standard of living and then stop. A shopkeeper in Damascus, for example, may keep open until he has earned the quota for the day and then go home, but a Western man feels disgraced if he retires before the day is done. This sense of shame goes beyond the attitude of the merchant adventurer like Jacob Fugger, who declined to retire because he enjoyed the game. The spirit of capitalism looks upon labor rather as a burden which is not to be laid down while yet there is strength, quite without regard to the meeting of any particular needs. The only counterpart in modern times is the furious drive of Communism which has made demonic workers out of the lackadaisical Russians.

What is the relation of religion, and notably Protestantism, to this whole development? If capitalism be defined in terms of lending, credit, banking, and bookkeeping, then the entire process is inseparable from the finances of the Catholic Church which utilized extensively the services of the Italian and German banking houses, notably the great moneylenders such as the Welsers and the Fuggers. But if capitalism be defined as an attitude to life marked by unremitting toil, then Protestantism is frequently held to have been not only congenial to the mood but indeed to have been its very originator. The major share is commonly credited to Calvinism, though Lutheranism is held also to have placed certain stones in the arch.⌐

⌐The Lutheran contribution is seen first in the rejection of monasticism and the exaltation of the common occupations as the appropriate spheres in which to serve God acceptably. The term *vocation* was transferred by Luther from the cloister to the workshop. The expression "vocational guidance" in its modern usage stems directly from him. In his eyes the occupations of the farmer, the doctor, the school teacher, the minister, the magistrate, the housemother, the maidservant and the manservant were all of them religious callings, vocations in which one was bound to render no lip service but to work diligently as serving not merely an earthly but also a heavenly master. The net result was to produce a morale for industry, not any fury of work, nor any disparagement of diversion, but a sense of duty in giving an honest day's toil. This attitude readily carried over from the farm to the factory and provided the entrepreneur with productive wage earners.

Another corollary of the rejection of monasticism was the attachment of a stigma to idleness and begging and to any parasitism upon the community. Here one must bear in mind that monasticism was itself a complex phenomenon, marked by varying phases. Throughout the Middle Ages the monastic rules had glorified manual labor for the monk, but at the same time the monasteries became the recipients of alms to a degree which dispensed with the necessity for work. Luther at the very moment when he destroyed monasticism was reverting to the original Benedictine exaltation of labor and was seeking to transfer it to all walks of life. At the same time he sought by excluding all mendicancy to forestall the corruptions which repeatedly overtook monasti- cism. Those who could work should work, and those who could not should be supported, but none should beg.

A further factor was an altered view of the propriety of charity. In the Middle Ages almsgiving was regarded as a good work, ministering to the salvation of the donor regard- less of the effect upon the recipient. Luther demolished the entire concept of saving oneself by good work and thereby eliminated the great popular motive for charity. Not the salvation of one's own soul but the assistance of the neighbor was the only defensible ground. For that reason charity should not be indiscriminate and might better be adminis- tered by organizations such as municipalities or churches rather than by individuals unable to pursue the social con- sequences. The total effect of these measures was to instill a spirit of economic self-reliance which made one reluctant to appeal for help save in dire necessity. There was no shred left of the feeling that one was really conferring a benefit through begging by providing another with an op- portunity to effect his salvation. Each was on his own. Poverty was either a misfortune or a disgrace, never a virtue. Parasitism was one of the deadly sins. Once more this is not to say that work became man's sole endeavor, but cer- tainly labor in common occupations was given a more exalted status.

In every other respect, however, Luther was conservative. He lived amid and loved an agrarian economy devoid of commerce and luxury. If he decried idleness and poverty, he deplored ostentation and luxury. He was quite Fran- ciscan in his own refusal to take any royalties from his prolific and lucrative publications. On one occasion, passing with a friend the palatial residence of a Wittenberg printer, Luther remarked, "I built that house." Luther discountenanced the taking of usury and was in this as in other regards more conservative than the Catholicism of his own day.

✳The question of the legitimacy of usury plays a large part in all of the discussions of the roles of Catholicism and Protestantism in the sixteenth century, and requires therefore a word of explanation. The great schoolmen, particularly Thomas Aquinas, allowed a contract of mutual risk but denied a contract of fixed return. The point was that the lender as well as the borrower might properly share in profit, provided both equally assumed the risk of loss. The objectionable practice was that Shylock should receive his ducats at a fixed rate and on a certain day, even though the ships of Antonio were on the rocks. But the Church of Luther's day was so extensively engaged in the business of borrowing at fixed interest rates that the Thomistic theory could not long survive. By the middle of the century the popes were expending between 50 and 60 per cent of their income to pay the interest on loans. Leo X of the Florentine merchant house of Medici lifted the ban on usury and John Eck, Luther's great theological opponent, went to Bologna at the expense of the Fuggers in order to defend the contract of fixed return against the contract of mutual risk.

In this area Luther was still a Thomist. Like Aquinas, he accepted the Aristotelian principle of the sterility of money, which as a matter of fact is valid in an agrarian economy where lending is for consumption rather than for production. Luther, who dwelt in a farming community, likened usury to the demand that a peasant return not only the goose which he had borrowed but also the eggs. His preference

was that all should live by labor rather than by lending.
His formula for those incapable of labor was community
support, but he applied this strictly only to the incapacitated
and made an exception in the case of the aged in possession
of funds capable of investment. Such people might live
on interest or usury provided however the rate did not exceed 5 per cent and provided likewise that the venture of
the borrower prospered. In other words this was the Thomistic contract of mutual risk. Luther's only departure from
medieval theory was in regarding the Deuteronomic prohi-
bition of usury as a local law of the Jewish commonwealth.
The question for Christians should be determined not by
the law of Moses but by the natural law principle of equity.

Calvin is often portrayed as having gone beyond Luther
in that he rejected also the theory of Aristotle, but the difference in practice from Luther or even Aquinas was
negligible. Calvin too stipulated that the rate should not
exceed 5 per cent and that there should be no return in
case of loss. The contract was still one of mutual risk.

Whether or no Protestantism or Catholicism be considered
to have done the more to stimulate capitalism by condoning
usury depends on the relative weight to be assigned to theory
and practice. The Catholic casuists like Eck retained the
authority of Deuteronomy and Aristotle and circumvented
the conclusions by ingenious interpretation. Luther dropped
one authority and Calvin both, yet retained the practice on
the basis of a different theoretical defense. One may properly ask whether those who broke down the practice were
not the more subversive.

A very famous and all too uncritically accepted thesis is
that Calvin, and Calvinism, provided that attitude toward
life which emerged as the spirit of capitalism, characterized

by demonic labor with no scruples as to the propriety of gain and with an aversion to the squandering of energy or the dispersal of wealth in enjoyment, with the result that, as charity diminished, the only outlet for accumulated funds was reinvestment in the business. Two ingredients in Calvin's ethos are held to have been responsible for the outcome. One is the duty of unremitting toil, the other a reluctance to expend either time or money in diversion.

The Calvinist devotion to work is explained by some on psychological grounds. It is said to be something more than the Lutheran teaching of the obligation to render faithful service in a calling. Rather it is a way of convincing oneself that one is of the elect. This was a problem about which John Calvin evinced no concern. In fact he considered preoccupation with one's own personal destiny to be unworthy. All this should be left to God with complete acquiescence. But such abnegation is claimed to have exceeded the capacities of his followers, who craved some assurance that they were of the chosen. They knew perfectly well that they could not earn their salvation by any degree of striving and they were equally aware that no infallible rule could be devised for determining how one stood in God's eyes. But they discerned a certain indicator in that mode of behavior which must issue from a state of election, and if this demeanor were present the assumption was plausible that the state of grace was its source. [Hence the impulse to work, not in order to earn salvation but to be assured of it. And if labor, then, were blessed by prosperity, one might infer a further sign of God's good pleasure.]

The taut endeavor was at no point to be relaxed by diversion. This was not the colossal striving of the merchant buccaneer who for all his magnificent spurts had no aversion

Merchants

to the delights of the flesh. The Calvinists are claimed to have been marked by an ascetic attitude to life, which, since monasticism had been repudiated, could express itself only in a rigorous discipline in the midst of ordinary occupations: hence methodical work with no dissipation of energy in amusement and no dispersal of wealth in luxury. For one with this outlook wealth could find no channel save to seek its own and pile up capital.

This is the picture offered of the Calvinist mood that provided a morale alike for the diligent worker and the enterprising employer both of whom might convince themselves of their election by incessant toil.

As a portrayal of Calvinism this delineation is open to criticism. In the first place nearly all of the citations adduced by way of proof are taken from English Puritanism rather than from early continental Calvinism. And in the second place proof in the nature of the case is elusive, because the modern analyst is seeking to bare hidden motives of which the participants could not be expected to have been aware. But the thesis does not wholly elude testing. There is absolutely no question that John Calvin worked himself to a wraith and there is equally no question that he was not worried about his salvation. Hence in his case the motive for industry cannot have been an effort to convince himself of his own predestination. His avowed motive for activity was to glorify God and to erect his kingdom. The same motivation is sufficient to account for the zeal of his followers. Their fundamental concern was not psychological and self-centered but theological and God-centered. The Eternal had written a drama in which they were to be the actors.

Moreover, in so far as some of them declined from Calvin's

exalted indifference to personal destiny, in so far as they may have sought psychological assurance, the test was emphatically not economic activity as such but rather upright character in every walk of life. The emphasis was much more on integrity than profit. Again worldly success as a proof of divine favor is simply not Calvinist whether for Calvin or for his followers. They knew how to be abased and they knew how to abound. They knew that the Lord chasteneth those whom he loveth. If one does find an interpretation of the flourishing of the vine and the fig tree as a reward for righteousness and a proof of divine favor there Calvinism has ceased to be Calvinism and Puritanism is no longer Puritanism.

The ascetic attitude toward worldly pleasures of which the current thesis makes much has been grossly overemphasized. Discipline is a better word than asceticism. The early Calvinists were not ethical rigorists. They did not eschew playing bowls or drinking wine. But there is no question that they were disciplined and it is true that work for them was itself a diversion. They had so much to do. Their task was so momentous that they begrudged every minute devoted to anything extraneous. They were out to erect God's kingdom upon earth. Diversion was diverting.

There can be no question, however, that, whatever the motivation, Calvinists did work, and they were perfectly willing to work in the economic sphere. And if they happened to be operating under an incipient capitalist economy, they gave to it the same impetus which they contributed to any other form of activity or economic organization. In early New England the Calvinists were confronted with the task not of introducing an industrial revolution but of subduing a wilderness. The economy at the start was exceedingly primitive. They devoted themselves to the erection of a holy commonwealth on a stern and rockbound coast, with a tenacity and a success which have driven modern secular historians to exclaim that surely the hand of God must have been in this and faith must be the most potent ingredient in survival.

Faith when it operates in the economic area engenders all of the economic virtues, industry, sobriety, honesty, and frugality, which invariably advance their possessors in the economic scale. What is this if it be not the old law, long since formulated by the medieval monk, that "discipline begets abundance, and abundance, unless we take the utmost care, destroys discipline; and discipline in its fall pulls down abundance"? The process was only intensified in Calvinism because the discipline arose from the faith that God had a great work to do within the historical process and that men had no other task than to glorify him by serving as the instruments of his purpose. As for the decline, that too ensued. The day was to come when Calvinism degenerated into methodical habits and prudential maxims, but it is not to the debacle that one should turn for an explanation of the spirit of capitalism.

As for the preference of Calvinists for industry rather than agriculture, this was largely a matter of circumstance. Luther's Saxony was a breadbasket. Calvin's Geneva was a port on the Rhone with trade relations to the north with the Swiss and to the south with the French by way of Lyons. Furthermore the thousands of refugees who poured into Geneva not infrequently were able to salvage their resources in the form of currency available for investment, and Calvin's refusal to restrict the right of lending at interest to the aged may find its explanation in the circumstance that he had on his hands so many of all ages who needed some-how or other to be made self-sustaining. Another great stronghold of Calvinism was the Netherlands, and this had long been the mart of Christendom, before ever the Calvin-ists entered the land.

Another factor to be taken into account is the role of religious refugees in the process of economic development. There were many such in the sixteenth century: the Italian and Spanish colonies in Geneva; the Locarno congregation which was transplanted to Zurich; English refugees at Frank-furt, Strasbourg, and Geneva; and Dutch refugees in great numbers in England. These people, like all the dislocated, had to be enterprising in order to survive. At one point they accelerated the development of capitalist organization quite apart from the question of a capitalist spirit. They had to be economic individualists. The countries to which they went both welcomed and feared them. The new skills which they introduced were prized but their competition with local workmen was feared. Hence they were not admitted to the ancient craft guilds, and had to set up for themselves. There-by obviously economic individualism was fostered.

Hence one may say that Calvinism has contributed to the spirit of capitalism only if it be added that Calvinism has injected a spirit of vitality and drive into every area in which Calvinists have been disposed to enter. They have exhibited unceasing endeavor whether they were subduing a conti-nent, overthrowing a monarchy, or managing a business, or again reforming the evils of the very order which they helped to create. Calvinists have been a strenuous breed.

In domestic relations Protestantism introduced the great-est change by dethroning virginity from a position of peculiar honor. The Catholic Church holds the paradoxical position that marriage is a sacrament, which the vow of celibacy is not, yet at the same time virginity is superior to marriage. This the Protestants roundly denied. Monasticism and clerical celibacy were alike abolished and the marriage state was exalted by way of compensation above the unmarried. A further consequence of the extinction of monasticism was the elevation of the home as the area where the gospel precepts can most readily be exemplified. There was no pretense on the part of Luther that perfection could be achieved anywhere; yet in the home there is no mine nor thine, and although the father exercises authority and is comparable to a magistrate, yet he does not wield the sword. In practice the home was the only sphere in which Lutheranism achieved any revolution in attitudes. Politics and business proved much less amenable to permeation. The pious household, where the father was priest as well as magistrate, where family prayers and the recital of the catechism were daily exercises — this picture marked for centuries the Lutheran household.

But this is not to say that Lutheran teaching at the outset meant any refinement in the relations of the sexes. Quite the contrary, because Luther in his polemic against the papacy at first laid the emphasis on the physical aspects of matrimony in order to prove that the pope in enjoining clerical celibacy was seeking to control the uncontrollable. The sexual impulse was declared to be as little subject to restraint as the urge to eat and to drink. Luther in saying this belied his own practice, for he had been chaste until his marriage in his forty-second year. After his marriage his tone shifted, and his concern was much less to establish the necessity of marriage than to portray the home as a school for character. In this sense it was for him a substitute for the monas-

Von dem Eelichen

Leben .D.M. Luther
Durch ine gepredigt
M.D XXij.

TITLE PAGE OF LUTHER'S TRACT ON MARRIAGE

tery. All of the vexations of domesticity, the tension of the sexes, the plague of bawling babies, and of disobedient children led him to say that there is no need to go hunting for crosses. At the same time he was often lyrical over the consolations of the married state.

Of any romantic picture of marriage there is no trace in early Protestantism. This was rather the work of the Renaissance adapting the ideals of the courts of love. They originated in southern France in the twelfth century as a reaction against the current concept of sexual relations as a sin rendered venial only through the sacrament of marriage, and of matrimony as a device for uniting families and transmitting properties. In complete rebellion the romantic picture declared love to be not a disease but an ennobling passion, possible only, however, outside the married state because love must be entirely unconstrained and freely bestowed without the least claim of one party upon the other. Romantic love was the cult of adultery. During the Renaissance the romantic notion began to fuse with marriage. One stage was the contention that if young people fall in love they should marry. The next step was to require that in order to marry they must first have fallen in love. The final step was to hold that if they ceased to be in love they should dissolve the marriage. Romanticism may thus both refine and destroy the marriage relationship. At neither point did it affect the Reformation. Luther's picture was completely unromantic. He himself married out of a sense of duty and he blamed Jacob for having worked seven years for the pretty face of Rachel when he already had Leah, though Luther was glad nevertheless that Jacob had done so because he thereby proved that he was saved by faith and not by works.

The problem of the dissolution of marriage in Catholic and Protestant ethics eventuated in well-marked discrepancies. The Catholic Church does not allow divorce but a practical equivalent is discovered in annulment. The view at that point has been sufficiently illustrated in the affair of Henry VIII. The practice of the Church in regarding even spiritual relations incurred by standing sponsor at baptisms and physical relations up to the seventh degree as impediments and then of granting dispensations was scorned by Luther as contemptible subterfuge, but he was entirely at one with the Catholic Church in prohibiting divorce. His own solution on occasion was bigamy. This he had suggested in the affair of Henry VIII on the ground that it had been practiced by the Old Testament patriarchs with divine approval and never expressly repudiated in the New Testament. Because of this advice the claim is often made that Protestantism broke down the moral restraints of the Catholic Church, but on that score both confessions were divided. The Swiss theologians, among them Zwingli, held that the previous dispensation was invalid and proposed annulment, whereas the pope, seeing that annulment was practically out of the question, himself suggested bigamy, and Cardinal Cajetan, Luther's great theological opponent, was entirely at one with him on the score of preferring bigamy to divorce.

The other case was that of the Protestant prince, Philip of Hesse, who at the age of nineteen was married for reasons of state to a wife for whom he felt an immediate aversion. He fell at once into habits of promiscuity which disturbed his conscience. He believed that he could contain himself if he had one wife to whom he was attached, and he consulted the Lutheran divines, who conceded bigamy with the stipulation that it should not be public in order not to flout the law. Philip proclaimed the event and scandal ensued. The modern solution would have been divorce and remarriage. The initial evil was the prostitution of marriage to political exigencies. One curious aspect of the whole situation is that Philip had to make an abject plea for pardon to the Emperor Charles V, whose several natural children were legitimatized by the pope and assumed important political posts. Charles V for his irregularities never suffered as did Philip of Hesse for breaking the law. Protestantism was soon to cut marital knots by more direct methods. Divorce was allowed by the Reformed churches and by the Anabaptists for other causes than adultery. The primary cause was diversity of faith. The Anabaptists would not tolerate mixed marriages, and if only one party joined their ranks the union was declared dissolved with freedom to remarry within the society in case the other remarried without. The same principle became operative in a more restricted way in Calvinism. If one party refused to follow the other into exile for the sake of the gospel, then the union was terminated. There was for example the case of the Marquis of Vico whose wife would not come to live with him in heretical Geneva. The conditions for living together simply did not exist. Catholics were not allowed to practice their religion in Geneva. The Marquis could not return to Italy, for there he would die at the stake. Under such circumstances the Calvinist pastors granted a divorce and he remarried.

The emphasis upon unity of faith within the marriage bond did much to foster another attitude toward matrimony which may be expressed in the term *partnership*. The stress was not upon marriage as a remedy for sin, nor upon the home as a school for character. Of any romantic touch there was not a trace. The centrality of faith made first for independence between husband and wife. Each must live by his or her own faith and not by that of the partner. But if that faith did exist in them both, then a basis existed for partnership in marriage, not merely in the propagation of children but in training them in the fear of the Lord and in laboring together in other respects for the glory of God and the advancement of his kingdom. This partnership is even more noteworthy among the Anabaptists where a missionary charge was laid upon every member of the community. Marriage in the Calvinist-Anabaptist tradition has been refined not through a cult of love but by focusing interest upon a common religious vocation.

To close merely by observing the effects of the Reformation on politics, economics and domestic relations may be quite misleading, because all these were only by-products. The Reformation was a religious revival. Its attempt was to give man a new assurance in the presence of God and a new motivation in the moral life. How far it succeeded no one can ever tell. Nothing is so interior as faith. Nothing is so elusive as piety. Chorales and hymns are a partial witness, but to know their force one must share with a congregation in song and prayer and look upon the faces of those who have no words with which to voice the innermost movings of their hearts This only one can say, that the Reformation at once rent and bound. The external unities were shattered, but the Christian consciousness of Europe was renewed. The Catholic Church itself was stimulated to carry through with accelerated pace the work already initiated by Ximenes. If there is still surviving any consciousness of Christian culture in the West, the Reformation of the sixteenth century is one of those periodic renewals to which it is due.

Bibliography

I. BIBLIOGRAPHICAL AIDS

Bainton, Roland H., *Bibliography of the Continental Reformation: Materials Available in English* (1935).

Church History carries bibliographical articles on phases of the Reformation, to wit:

Pauck on the German Reformation (Dec., 1940); Huber on the Catholic Church in the Renaissance (March, 1941); Krahn on the Mennonites in the Netherlands (September, 1944); McNeill on Calvin (Dec., 1949); Bard Thompson on Zwingli (June, 1950); Dillenberger on Luther (June, 1956); Tavard on Catholic Reform (Sept., 1957); George Williams on the Anabaptists and Spiritual Reformers (March and June, 1958).

Current literature is covered in the following periodicals: *Church History;* the *Mennonite Quarterly Review;* and the *Archiv für Reformationsgeschichte* (articles and reviews in English and German).

II. ENCYCLOPEDIAS

The Encyclopaedia Britannica. The eleventh edition of 1910-11 was superior to the fourteenth of 1929.

The Encyclopedia of Religion and Ethics (1908-27), has articles on "The Reformation" and on the leading varieties.

The Encyclopedia of the Social Sciences (1930-35), has a few choice articles, e.g. on Luther, Castellio, Franck and Muentzer.

The New Schaff-Herzog Encyclopedia of Religious Knowledge, 12 vols. (1908-12), is the best for the Reformation. Reprint (1951), Supplement, 2 vols. (1955).

The Mennonite Encyclopedia, 3 vols. (1955).

III. GENERAL SURVEYS

The Cambridge Modern History, Vol. II (*The Reformation,* 1958), contains a series of essays by various authors

Lindsay, Thomas M., *A History of the Reformation,* 2 vols. (1916, 1917). Despite its age this work is still very useful because of the scope of the treatment and the theological interest.

Smith, Preserved, *The Age of the Reformation* (1920). The first half is devoted to a sketch of the Reformation by countries, the second to a discussion of social and cultural conditions, in which the author was more interested than in theological aspects.

Mosse, G. K., *The Reformation* (Berkshire Studies, 1953). Brief.

Grimm, Harold, *The Reformation Era* (1934). Particularly fine for the political events.

Harbison. E. H., *The Age of the Reformation* (1955). Brief, illuminating.

Bainton, Roland H., *The Age of the Reformation* (Anvil, 1956). Mainly documentary.

IV. LUTHER AND THE GERMAN REFORMATION

A. Luther's work in translation:

Jacobs, H. E., ed., *Works of Martin Luther*, 6 vols. (1915-32).

Smith, P., and Gallinger, H. P., *Conversations with Luther* (1915).

Smith, P., *Luther's Correspondence*, 2 vols. (1913-18).

The Concordia Publishing House and the Muhlenberg Press are jointly bringing out a fifty-five volume edition of Luther's works in English translation. Four volumes are now available.

B. On Luther:

Protestant biographies:

Bainton, R. H., *Here I Stand: A Life of Martin Luther* (1950).

Boehmer, H., *Road to Reformation*, 1946. German Lutheran; takes Luther up to 1521.

Fife, Robert H., *The Revolt of Martin Luther* (1957). Very detailed.

Koestlin, J. T., *Life of Luther*, 1893. German Lutheran; old but not superseded for comprehensiveness in small scope.

Kooimann, W. J., *By Faith Alone* (1955). Popular.

Mackinnon, James, *Luther and the Reformation*, 4 vols. (1925-30). Presbyterian; detailed.

McGiffert, A. C., *Martin Luther* (1917). Liberal Protestant; popular.

Smith, Preserved, *Life and Letters of Martin Luther* (1911). Liberal Protestant; copious use of letters.

Schwiebert, Ernest G., *Luther and His Times* (1950). Especially valuable for the role of the University of Wittenberg.

Catholic biographies:

Denifle, H., *Luther and Lutherdom* (1917). Vilification.

Febvre, L., *Martin Luther: A Destiny* (1919). Reviews Catholic scholarship.

Grisar, H., *Luther*, 6 vols. (1913-17).

———, *Martin Luther*, 1 vol. (1930). Disparaging of Luther.

Special phases:

Carlson, Edgar M., *The Reinterpretation of Luther* (1948). Surveys Swedish studies.

Dillenberger, John, *God Hidden and Revealed*, the interpretation of Luther's *Deus absconditus* (1953).

Forell, G. W., *Faith Active in Love* (1954). Luther's social ethic.

Luther Today (1957). Essays by Quanbek, Rupp and Bainton.

Reu, Michael, *Luther's German Bible* (1934). The appendix translates portions of the lectures on Romans.

————, *The Augsburg Confession* (1930). Translates many important documents.

Rupp, E. G., *Luther's Progress to the Diet of Worms* (1951).

————, *The Righteousness of God* (1953). Admirable.

Watson, Philip S., *Let God Be God* (1947). Luther's theology.

C. On other leaders:

Eells, Hastings, *Martin Bucer* (1931).

Holborn, Hajo, *Ulrich von Hutten* (1935).

Manschreck, Clyde, *Melanchthon* (1958).

Ruccius, W., "John Bugenhagen," *Lutheran Church Review*, XLII (1923); XLIII (1924).

V. ZWINGLI AND THE REFORMATION IN GERMAN SWITZERLAND

The Latin Works and Correspondence (in English), ed. by S. M. Jackson, 3 vols. (1912-29).

Selected Works, ed. by S. M. Jackson (1901).

Selected Works of Zwingli and Bullinger, ed. Bromiley (Christian Classics, XXIV, 1953).

Jackson, S. M., *Huldreich Zwingli* (1901).

Farner, Oskar, *Zwingli the Reformer* (1952).

VI. CALVIN AND GENEVA

A. Calvin's works in translation:

Works, published by the Calvin Translation Society. *The Institutes* are particularly important.

B. Calvin and Calvinism:

Breen, Q., *John Calvin: A Study in French Humanism* (1931).

Harkness, Georgia, *John Calvin: The Man and His Ethics* (1932). A study mainly of the economic ethics.

Hunt, R. M. C., *Calvin* (1933). Useful.

Reyburn, H. Y., *John Calvin* (1914). Full, readable.

Walker, W., *John Calvin* (1906). Still the best succinct statement.

Baird, Henry M., *Theodore Beza, the Counsellor of the French Reformation, 1519-1605* (1899).

McNeill, John T., *The History and Character of Calvinism* (1954).

C. Phases of Calvin's Thought:

Davies, R. E., *The Problem of Authority in the Continental Reformers* (1946).
Dowey, Edward A., *The Knowledge of God in Calvin's Theology* (1952).
Hunter, A. M., *The Teaching of Calvin* (1950).
Niesel, William, *The Theology of Calvin* (1956).
Parker, T. H. L., *The Doctrine of the Knowledge of God: A Study in the Theology of John Calvin* (1952).
Quistorp, H., *Calvin's Doctrine of Last Things* (1955).
Torrance, T. F., *Calvin's Doctrine of Man* (1949).
Wallace, R. S., *Calvin's Doctrine of the Word and Sacrament* (1953).

VII. THE ANABAPTISTS

A. Definitions:

Bainton, R. H., "The Left Wing of the Reformation," *Journal of Religion*, XXI (April, 1941).
Friedmann, Robert, "Conception of the Anabaptists," *Church History*, IX (Dec., 1940).
Jones, Rufus, "The Anabaptists," *Harvard Theological Review*, XI (1918).

B. Sources:

Van Braght, T., *A Martyrology*, 2 vols. (1850-53).
The Complete Works of Menno Simons (1956).
Spiritual and Anabaptist Writers, ed. George Williams (Christian Classics, XXV, 1957).

C. Studies:

Bax, Belfort, *Rise and Fall of the Anabaptists* (1903). On the Münster episode.
Deets, L. E., *The Hutterites* (1939). Sociological.
Dosker, H. E., *The Dutch Anabaptists* (1921).
Hershberger, Guy F., *The Recovery of the Anabaptist Vision*, essays in honor of Harold Bender (1957).
Horsch, John, *The Mennonites in Europe* (1942).
———, *The Hutterian Brethren* (1931).
Jones, Rufus M., *Studies in Mystical Religion* (1909).
Kautsky, Karl, *Communism in Central Europe* (1897). Economic causation.
Littell, Franklin, *The Anabaptist View of the Church* (1958).
Mennonite Quarterly Review, XXIV (Jan., 1950). Special Anabaptist theology issue.
Smithson, R., *The Anabaptists* (1935).

D. Biographies:

Bender, Harold, *The Life and Letters of Conrad Grebel* (1950-).

Coutts, A., *Hans Denck* (1927).
Horsch, J., *Menno Simons* (1916).
Vedder, H. C., *Bathazar Huebmaier* (1905).
Weis, F. L., *The Life, Teachings and Works of Johannes Denck* (1924).
———, *The Life, Teachings and Works of Ludwig Hetzer* (1930).

VIII. FRANCE

Baird, H. M., *History of the Rise of the Huguenots of France*, 2 vols. (1879).
———, *The Huguenots and Henry of Navarre*, 2 vols. (1886).
———, *The Huguenots and the Revocation of the Edict of Nantes*, 2 vols. (1895). Solid.
The Cambridge Modern History, Vol. III: *The Wars of Religion* (1904).
Kelly, C. G., *French Protestantism 1559-62* (1918).
Kingdon, Robert, *Geneva and the Coming of the Wars of Religion* (1956).
Palm, F. C., *Calvinism and the Religious Wars* (1932).
———, *Politics and Religion in Sixteenth Century France* (1927).
Thompson, J. W., *The Wars of Religion in France* (1909).
Tilley, A. A., *The French Wars of Religion* (1919). Introduction to the literature.
White, H., *The Massacre of St. Bartholomew* (1868).
Whitehead, A. W., *Gaspard de Coligny* (1904).
Zopf, Otto, *The Huguenots* (1942).

IX. ITALY

A. Sources:

Many of the writings of Juan Valdes have been translated, some by Benjamin Wiffin, some by John T. Betts.

B. General surveys:

Brown, G. K., *Italy and the Reformation to 1550* (1933).
Church, Frederic C., *The Italian Reformers 1534-64* (1932).

C. Biography:

Bainton, Roland H., *The Travail of Religious Liberty* (1951). Includes a discussion of Ochino.
Young, M., *The Life and Times of Aonio Paleario*, 2 vols. (1860).

X. SPAIN

Bochmer, E., *Bibliotheca Wiffeniana, Spanish Reformers of Two Centuries from 1520*, 3 vols., (1874, 1883, 1904).
Wilkens, C. A., *Spanish Protestants in the Sixteenth Century* (1897).

XI. NETHERLANDS

Harrison, F., *William the Silent* (1897).
Motley, H. L., *The Rise of the Dutch Republic,* 3 vols. (1856).
Putnam, Ruth, *William the Silent,* 2 vols. (1898).
Wedgewood, *William the Silent* (1944).

XII. SCANDINAVIA

Bergendorf, Conrad, *Olavus Petri . . . : A Study of the Swedish Reformation* (1928).
Gjerset, Knut, *History of the Norwegian People* (1932).
Wordsworth, John, *The National Church of Sweden* (1910).
Dunkley, E. H., *The Reformation in Denmark* (1948).

XIII. POLAND AND HUNGARY

Fox, P., *The Reformation in Poland* (1924).
History of the Protestant Church in Hungary, trans. by J. Craig (1854).
Krasinski, N., *Historical Sketch of the . . . Reformation in Poland,* 2 vols. (1834-40).
Kot, S., *Socinianism in Poland* (1957).

XIV. THE STRUGGLE FOR RECOGNITION AND LIBERTY

Bainton, R. H., *The Travail of Religious Liberty* (1951).
———, "The Struggle for Religious Liberty," *Church History,* X (June, 1941).
Evans, A. P., *An Episode in the Struggle for Religious Freedom* (1924).
Jordan, W. K., *The Development of Religious Toleration in England,* 4 vols. (1932-40).
Persecution and Liberty: Essays in Honor of G. L. Burr (1931).

XV. ENGLAND AND SCOTLAND

A. Background:

Arrowsmith, R. D., *Prelude to the Reformation* (1923). Decline of monasticism.
Marti, Oscar, *Economic Causes of the Reformation in England* (1929).
Smith, H. M., *Pre-Reformation England* (1938). Informative.

B. Sources:

Edward VI, *Prayer Book.*
Foxe, J., *Book of Martyrs.*
Gee, H., and Hardy, W. J., *Documents Illustrative of English Church History* (1914).
Knox, J., *Works,* ed. by Laing, 6 vols. (1846-64).
———, *History of the Reformation in Scotland.*

The Parker Society publications, 55 vols. (1943-55).
The works of John Strype, 23 vols. (1821-40).

C. General Surveys:

In one or two volumes:

Carter, S. C., *The English Church and the Reformation* (1925). Readable.

Clark, W., *The Anglican Reformation* (1897). Anglican.

Constant, G., *The Reformation in England,* 2 vols. (1934-42). Catholic; very satisfactory.

Maitland, S. R., *The Reformation in England* (1906). Entertaining excerpts.

Parker, T. M., *The English Reformation to 1558* (1950).

Rupp, E. G., *Studies in the Making of the English Protestant Tradition* (1947).

In several volumes:

Burnet, G., *The History of the Reformation in England,* ed. by Nicholas Pocock, 7 vols. (1865).

Dixon, R. W., *History of the Church of England,* 6 vols. (1895-1902). Splendid.

Hughes, Philip, *The Reformation in England,* 3 vols. (1952-54). Decidedly Catholic.

D. Special aspects:

Baskerville, G., *English Monks and the Suppression of the Monasteries* (1937).

Baumer, F., *Early Tudor Theory of Kingship* (1940).

———, "The Church of England and the Common Corps of Christendom," *Journal of Modern History,* XVI (March, 1944).

Davies, E. T., *Episcopacy and the Royal Supremacy in the Church of England in the Sixteenth Century* (1950).

Fletcher, J. S., *The Reformation in Northern England* (1925).

Garrett, C. H., *The Marian Exiles* (1938).

Gasquet, F. A., *Henry VIII and the English Monasteries* (1893).

Hague, D., *The Story of the English Prayer Book* (1926).

Lacey, T. A., *The Reformation and the People* (1929). Anglo-Catholic.

Norwood, F. A., *The Reformation Refugees as an Economic Force* (1942).

Pollard, A. F., *England Under the Protector Somerset* (1900).

Rose-Troup, F., *The Western Rebellion of 1549* (1913).

White, H. C., *Social Criticism in Popular Religious Literature of the Sixteenth Century* (1944).

Whitney, E. A., "Erastianism and Divine Right," *Huntington Library Quarterly* (Jan., 1939).

Wright, L., "The Significance of Religious Writings in the English Renaissance," *Journal of the History of Ideas,* I (Jan., 1940).

E. Biography:
>   Chambers, R. W., *Thomas More* (1935).
>   Cowan, H., *John Knox* (1905). Sympathetic, thorough.
>   Deane, A. C., *Life of Thomas Cranmer* (1927). Disparaging.
>   Demaus, R., *Hugh Latimer* (reprinted 1927).
>   ———, *William Tyndale* (reprinted 1927).
>   Lee, Maurice, *James Stewart* (1953).
>   MacGregor, Geddes, *Thundering Scot: A Portrait of John Knox* (1957). Lively.
>   Muller, J. A., *Stephen Gardiner* (1926). Study of a Tudor conservative.
>   Percy, E., *John Knox* (1937). Fine insights.
>   Pollard, A. F., *Henry VIII* (1905).
>   ———, *Thomas Cranmer* (1904). Solid.
>   ———, *Wolsey* (1929).
>   Smyth, C. H. E., *Cranmer* (1926). Defends his doctrinal consistency.

XVI. THE FREE SPIRITS

>   Bainton, R. H., *Sebastian Castellio and the Toleration Controversy* (1935).
>   ———, *Hunted Heretic: The Life and Death of Michael Servetus* (1953).
>   Jones, R. M., *Spiritual Reformers in the Sixteenth and Seventeenth Centuries* (1914).
>   Wilbur, E. M., *A History of Unitarianism*, Vol. I (1945).

XVII. POLITICAL ASPECTS

>   Allen, J. W., *A History of Political Thought in the Sixteenth Century* (1928).
>   Foster, H. W., "The Political Theories of Calvinists . . . ," *American Historical Review*, XXI (1915).
>   Murray, R. H., *The Political Consequences of the Reformation* (1926).
>   Reynolds, Beatrice, *Proponents of Limited Monarchy* (1931).

XVIII. ECONOMIC AND SOCIAL ASPECTS

>   Ehrenberg, Richard, *Capital and Finance in the Age of the Renaissance* (n.d.).
>   Nelson, B. N., *The Idea of Usury* (1949).
>   Pascal, R., *The Social Basis of the German Reformation* (1933).
>   Tawney, R. H., *Religion and the Rise of Capitalism* (1926).
>   Weber, Max, *The Protestant Ethic and the Spirit of Capitalism* (1930).

XIX. INTERPRETATION

>   McGiffert, A. C., *Protestant Thought Before Kant* (1911).
>   Pauck, Wilhelm, *The Heritage of the Reformation* (1950).
>   Troeltsch, Ernst, *The Social Teaching of the Christian Churches*, 2 vols. (English translation 1949).

SUPPLEMENTARY BIBLIOGRAPHY

Elton, G. R., ed. *The Reformation.* Volume 2 of *The New Cambridge Modern History.* Cambridge, 1962.

Hillerbrand, Hans J. *A Bibliography of Anabaptism, 1520-1630.* Elkhart, Ind., 1962.

Jedin, Hubert. *A History of the Council of Trent.* Saint Louis, 1957—.

Manns, Peter. *Martin Luther: An Illustrated Biography.* Introduction by Jaroslav Pelikan. New York, 1982.

Oakley, Francis. *The Western Church in the Later Middle Ages.* Ithaca, 1979.

Oberman, Heiko A. *The Harvest of Medieval Theology: Gabriel Biel and Late Medieval Nominalism.* Cambridge, Mass., 1963.

———. *Masters of the Reformation: The Emergence of a New Intellectual Climate in Europe.* Cambridge, 1981.

Ozment, Steven E., ed. *The Reformation in Medieval Perspective.* Chicago, 1971.

———. *The Age of Reform, 1250-1550: An Intellectual and Religious History of Late Medieval and Reformation Europe.* New Haven, 1980.

McConica, James, et al., eds. *Collected Works of Erasmus.* Toronto, 1974—.

Pelikan, Jaroslav, and Lehmann, Helmut T., eds. *Luther's Works: American Edition.* Saint Louis and Philadelphia, 1955—.

Pelikan, Jaroslav. *Reformation of Church and Dogma (1300-1700).* Volume 4 of *The Christian Tradition: A History of the Development of Doctrine.* Chicago, 1984.

Spitz, Lewis W. *The Religious Renaissance of the German Humanists.* Cambridge, Mass., 1963.

Williams, George Huntston. *The Radical Reformation.* Philadelphia, 1962.

Index